MIND AT PLAY

MIND AT PLAY

THE PSYCHOLOGY OF

VIDEO GAMES

GEOFFREY R. LOFTUS

&

ELIZABETH F. LOFTUS

Basic Books, Inc., Publishers　　　　　*New York*

Library of Congress Cataloging in Publication Data

Loftus, Geoffrey R., 1945–
  Mind at play.

  Includes bibliographical references and index.
  1. Video games—Psychological aspects. 2. Video
games. I. Loftus, Elizabeth F., 1944–
II. Title.
GV1469.3.L63   1983   794.8'2'019   83–70761
  ISBN 0–465–04069–6

This book is dedicated to

the memory of

RUSSELL LOFTUS

(1916–1982)

who, from the start of the project,

provided support, inspiration,

and provocative ideas.

CONTENTS

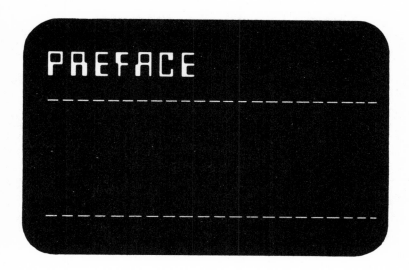

PREFACE

Our aim is to shed light on the intriguing phenomenon of video games. Along the way, we'll introduce some of the most far-ranging ideas in modern psychology and also provide an entrée to the world of computers, for the appeal of the games is largely psychological and video games owe their very existence to the computer revolution.

When we set out to write a book on the psychology of video games, we tried to adopt a relatively neutral stance. We read everything we could about the games. We went to video arcades to play the games and to talk to the owners, players, and onlookers. We talked to parents and critics. At the same time, we explored the contributions that research in psychology might provide for an understanding of the games.

After we had poked around for a while, some themes began to emerge. A major one was the computer theme: video games are fundamentally different from all other games in history because of the computer technology that underlies them. The marriage of games and computers has produced both costs and benefits. It enables, for example, the design of games that are extremely compelling to play. Critics would call the games addictive. Proponents would call them great fun.

A second theme involves ability. Playing a video game requires intricately tuned skills. How are these skills acquired? What are the mental components that go into them?

A final theme revolves around education. We believe that the games combine two ingredients—intrinsic motivation and computer-based interaction—that make them potentially the most powerful educational tools ever invented. We have discovered, much to our delight, a number of research projects that are striving to harness this educational power. Some are succeeding. More will succeed in the coming years.

While writing this book, we've had help from a variety of people who deserve special thanks. Craig Raglund provided a number of perceptive suggestions about the potential uses of video games in education. Hank Samson and Jim Diaz, who are much better players than we've yet become, engaged us in lively discussions about reinforcement. Ellen Markman, Delia Gerhardt, and Brian Wandell read and provided useful comments on early versions of several chapters. And, finally, there's no way to adequately thank Judy Greissman, our editor at Basic Books, who initiated the whole idea and who did a magnificent job shepherding it through all stages from start to finish.

Geoffrey R. Loftus

Elizabeth F. Loftus

MIND AT PLAY

CHAPTER 1

VIDEOMANIA

Venturing into a video arcade, you find a decidedly mixed crowd. To be sure, most players are "typical teenagers," who play the video games for at least a few hours every week.[1] But a not uncommon sight is the corporation executive, the housewife, the construction worker. According to one survey, about half the game players (in arcades and elsewhere) are over the age of twenty-six.[2]

The economics of the video game craze are staggering. Each year more than $5 billion is spent in the video arcades alone.[3] And while the video parlor operators are busily collecting their

[1]G. Gallup, "The Typical American Teen-ager," *Seattle Times*, 19 May 1982.
[2]A. Katz, "Switch On," *Electronic Games* 1 (May 1982): 6.
[3]D. Surrey, "It's, Like, Good Training for Life," *Natural History* 91 (November 1982): 71–83.

quarters, microcomputer manufacturers are expected to make similarly large sums selling both home computers and the software to go with them. Advertisements for home computers in traditional publications describe the virtues of keeping the checkbook balanced, maintaining Christmas card lists, and teaching the children to program. However, by far the major use of home computers is for video games, and indeed the potential home video game market provided a major incentive for the development of many home computers in the first place. Six or seven years ago hardly any video games existed. But today arcade and home video games comprise an industry that has reached over $7 billion.

While questioning people in the course of preparing this book, we uncovered a wide range of feelings about the games, most of them quite passionate. A twenty-three-year-old computer engineer, David, was playing portable video games non-stop on a flight we shared with him. "What do you like about these games?" we asked. His answer was quite definite: "I think they're entertaining. They fascinate me. I can't believe I can hold something almost as small as a credit card that can play a game I haven't mastered. They're a challenge. What's most intriguing is that I know because of my work that there is a pattern to these games. And I haven't yet figured it out. But I keep getting closer. I keep getting better."

On the other hand, Glen, a twenty-five-year-old property manager, hates video games. He says just as definitely: "I get no satisfaction out of beating a machine!" And Jane, a thirty-eight-year-old management consultant, sees them as a soporific for teenagers, an aesthetic nightmare, and is adamant that they are no good at all for anything whatsoever. The opinions of public figures reflect this controversy. The U.S. Surgeon General, Everett Koop, decries video games, while Isaac Asimov, one of the most respected science writers in the United States, extolls their educational benefits.[4]

Given these extreme differences of opinion, we find the job of trying to understand the video game explosion even more challenging.

Figure 1.1 shows the "family tree" of video games. Their immediate parents were the digital computer and the arcade game. The computer side of this parentage will be traced in chapter 6; the arcade side, in chapter 4.

Most games involve competition of one sort or another. But somewhere along the line, solitary games evolved, in which competition, if it even exists, is with yourself (for example, trying to top your previous best score) or with some abstract entity such as a deck of cards or a machine. Most video games are, or can be, solitary games. You play chiefly against the machine.

Three conceptual ingredients enter into the immediate background of video games:

1. *Sound and fury.* Flashing lights, bizarre noises, and continuously displayed, astronomical scores were incorporated in pinball machines. Often associated with sleazy bars and arcades and thought to be controlled by organized crime, nonetheless pinball machines managed to build up a mystique. They were colorful and gaudy. Presumably in an effort to give the illusion of variety, different games in an arcade represented an enormous variety of concepts, ranging from the Vietnam War to the Indianapolis 500 to the Playboy penthouse. However, all these games were virtually identical in terms of how they were played and what the goals were.

2. *Death and destruction.* In the 1960s a new kind of game

[4]I. Asimov, "The New Learning," *Videogaming Illustrated* 1 (October 1982): 16.

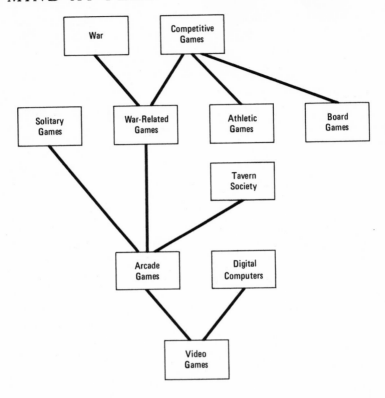

FIGURE 1.1

The family tree of video games.

began to compete with pinball for arcade space. These games were usually automated in some fairly sophisticated way and usually involved violence of one sort or another. In Bomber Pilot, for example, the player, after inserting a quarter, was seemingly placed at the controls of a bomb-laden jet plane and presented with varying terrain passing below. The goal was to drop bombs on targets that would appear for a few seconds beneath the aircraft and then vanish. Points were awarded for successful hits, with the highest numbers of points being awarded for the destruction of high-density population areas, such as large cities, and strategic targets, such as enemy missile bases. The player was constantly under threat of enemy antiaircraft fire and therefore had to worry about taking evasive action as well as aiming the bombs. Like pinball, these arcade games were supplemented by exotic flashing lights, violent noises, and rapidly increasing scores, which were prominently displayed.

3. *Computer control.* In the 1970s another game arrived, unobtrusively, on the scene. This newcomer, Pong, differed from its predecessors in several ways. First, and most important, it was entirely under the control of a computer, and except for the player's joysticks, there were no moving parts. Everything was electronic. In a major way, Pong heralded the dawn of a new era.

Pong's second distinction was that it somehow acquired an immediate, broad social acceptance. It suddenly appeared in all sorts of places—in cocktail lounges, train stations, airliners—where no one would dream of putting either pinball or the death and destruction games. Although the reasons for this broad social acceptance are not entirely clear, it is interesting to speculate. First, size doubtless played a part. The older games, which used heavy mechanical parts, were large and difficult to transport (and were certainly not welcome in places like airplanes where size and weight are at a premium). Pong, with a computer at its heart, was much more mobile. Second, in the years following its introduction, Pong's price—along with the prices of all other computer-based goods—fell rapidly, and thus the game became widely available. In fact, in the mid-1970s versions of Pong—primitive by today's standards, but revolutionary then—began to find their way into individual households. And, finally, Pong's central theme was not the violence and kitsch of the previous arcade games. Instead, it

7

mimicked the then-genteel racquet games such as tennis and squash. This feature may well have provided the lubrication necessary to ease the game into polite society.

For whatever reasons, Pong managed to escape from the smoky, seedy atmosphere of its pinball arcade predecessors, and it set the stage for the widespread status currently enjoyed by today's video games. As we have indicated, the computer basis of Pong, with its attendant implications for cost and mobility, was a critical ingredient of this transition. In chapter 6 we shall summarize the computer revolution and its critical role in the psychology of video games.

Throughout this book, we are going to take the theories and experiments of psychologists and use them to understand the video game phenomenon that has sent many children into video arcades and many parents into fits of nervousness. When the surgeon general marches through the country crying, in essence, "Warning. Video games may be hazardous to your children's health," should we believe him? Dr. Koop has argued that there is nothing constructive about the games and that in fact they may be teaching children to kill and destroy since that's what most of the games are about. In this book, however, we'll take the position that his fear may be completely unwarranted. Video games, at least in some form, are going to be with us for quite some time, and it is important to analyze dispassionately their psychological costs and their benefits. We should not ban video games without a deep and thoughtful analysis, any more than we should ban hopscotch or Monopoly.

When people ask "What good are these games, anyhow?" the suggestion is often heard that they have a direct benefit of increasing some skill like eye-hand coordination. But so do many activities, such as baseball and sewing. What are not usually considered are the indirect benefits that video games can and do yield. These can be quite unexpected and enormously powerful. We refer to such benefits as the creation of an intense interest in computers, which has led many of the game players of the early 1980s to jobs as computer programmers with major corporations. We interviewed one such man, Greg, who at the age of twenty-three had landed a programming job with a growing software company just south of San Francisco. Greg spends his days writing computer programs and claims he's happier than he has ever been in his life. Five years earlier, Greg's parents worried that he was spending too much time playing video games. They thought he might be "addicted" to the games the way other kids seemed to become addicted to drugs or alcohol. Now—five years later—they take tremendous pride in their son's work. They have come to realize that the games were the start of his intense interest in computers that led to his career.

What was it about video games that Greg found so appealing? Why was he willing to forgo sporting events and trips to the beach to spend time in video arcades? To address such questions, we now draw upon the field of psychology.

CHAPTER 2

WHY VIDEO GAMES ARE FUN

Syndicated columnist Ellen Goodman has described her own initiation into video games. One cloudy day she was waiting for an airplane in the Detroit airport. She had time on her hands and thought she would try a quick game of Pac-Man. Before she knew it, she was hooked; Pac-Man took her for every last quarter she had. It began innocently enough. She put in her first quarter but, not yet having a feel for the game, she shoved Pac-Man into the arms of the nearest monster. Undiscouraged by defeat, she tried again. She did a little better this time. Something about the game made her think she could win. So she kept at it. Fortunately for Goodman, she was able to break the habit before it broke her. Once she gained some distance —away from the clutches of Pac-Man—she thought about it clearly. "Pac-Man hooks only those people who confuse victory with slow defeat."[1]

Why do people find the games so compelling? In this chapter we will illustrate how the psychological concepts of reinforcement, cognitive dissonance, and regret help explain the process of video game addiction. Although very few psychological studies deal directly with the issue of why video games are fun, we found one that does. At the end of this chapter, we'll describe it.

Pac-Man, by Way of Example

In describing how experimental psychologists might view and explain video game behavior, it's useful to have one example to rely on throughout. Because it has been one of the most popular games, we've chosen Ellen Goodman's nemesis, Pac-Man. For the benefit of any readers who have been living somewhere besides Earth for the past few years, we'll provide a brief description of Pac-Man here.

The game Pac-Man gets its name from the Japanese term *paku paku,* which means "gobble gobble." The character Pac-Man is a little yellow creature who looks like he's smiling. He is set in a somewhat complex maze that's initially filled with yellow dots. The player controls Pac-Man's movements with a four-directional joystick or control knob, thereby allowing him to move left, right, up, or down. His jaw faces the direction in which he's moving.

As he glides around through the maze, Pac-Man gobbles up

[1]E. Goodman, "I Should Have Known He Was . . . Temptation," *Seattle Times,* 18 May 1982.

the dots. Simultaneously, however, he's vigorously pursued by four monsters (each a different color) named Inky, Blinky, Pinky, and Clyde. If one of the monsters catches him, Pac-Man slowly folds up and wilts away while the machine provides sympathetic noises. Pac-Man can be eaten only three times before the game ends, the score reverts to zero, and another quarter is required for further play.

Pac-Man has a variety of ways of combatting and outwitting the monsters. First, by adept maneuvering, he can keep away from them. Second, at each of the four corners of the board is a glowing, extra-strength dot called an energizer. Whenever Pac-Man eats an energizer, some, or all, of the monsters turn blue. When a monster is blue, contact between it and Pac-Man results in the monster's demise rather than in Pac-Man's. However, monsters remain blue only for brief periods following Pac-Man's consumption of an energizer; moreover, a monster destroyed by Pac-Man doesn't stay destroyed, but instead returns to action following a short interlude in the penalty box.

If Pac-Man eats all the dots in the maze, the player has completed a "board" and a new maze with fresh dots appears. This provision of new boards can continue indefinitely; however, with each successive board, things become more difficult. The monsters move faster and are blue for shorter periods of time; Pac-Man moves slower; and so on. In between each board, a short, amusing skit occurs on the screen.

When playing Pac-Man, the player is rewarded in many ways. For example, points are awarded for gobbling up the dots and for destroying monsters. Additionally, there is some symbol in the center of the board. What the symbol is depends on how many boards the player has managed to get through. For instance, a cherry appears on the first board, a strawberry on the second, until finally, a key appears on the twelfth board and all subsequent boards. Naturally, Pac-Man aficionados have memorized the sequence of symbols, and the symbols that signify that many boards have been accomplished are the most prestigious. The symbols themselves can be eaten by Pac-Man for progressively increasing numbers of points. And finally, additional sources of reinforcement are the amusing skits that occur between boards.

The first time you drop a quarter into a Pac-Man game, you might get a score of 1,000, if you're lucky. Less than a minute will pass, and your Pac-Man will be eaten three times in disconcertingly rapid succession. But chances are you'll play again. And again. And again. You might get through a couple of boards, and your score might get up to 5,000 or so. But what will puzzle you most is this: the top score for the day will be posted on the machine. It might be 56,000. Or 102,000. It could be over 500,000.

How could anyone get such a score? In the next chapter we'll focus on the mental and physical skills that go into video game facility. For the moment, however, let's concern ourselves with the question of how people become so motivated that they'll play video games hour after hour, day after day. To do so, we'll consider the phenomenon of reinforcement.

Mechanics of Reinforcement

On a clear Vermont night, a young boy sits methodically scanning the sky in search of shooting stars. In a sleazy Las Vegas casino, a glassy-eyed old woman mechanically deposits nickel after nickel in a slot machine. And in a posh Chicago suburb, a teenager spends hours playing Gallaxian at the video parlor every afternoon when school lets out.

These three situations have a common element: in each one,

behavior is dictated by what psychologists refer to as the partial reinforcement effect. To understand this effect—which is a critical psychological ingredient of video game addiction—it will be useful to provide a thumbnail sketch of reinforcement itself and the role it plays in shaping behavior. Video games are designed to take your money, and they have an uncanny way of doing so. They play on the ordinary person's weaknesses for reinforcement.

BASIC CONCEPTS

Reinforcement is the provision for you of something that you like. In each of the three preceding examples, reinforcement of some sort is involved. For the aspiring astronomer, seeing a shooting star is a reinforcement. For the Vegas gambler, the slot machine's payoff is a reinforcement. And for the video game player, beating a previous high score or winning a free game or shooting down enemy spaceships is a reinforcement. There are a variety of psychological theories designed to explain the role of reinforcement in behavior. Central to all of them, however, is the idea that any behavior that is followed by reinforcement will increase in frequency. In short, video games that do something to make a player feel good will be played again and again.

Certain elementary kinds of human behavior can be analyzed nicely by referring to well-studied principles of reinforcement. To get the complete picture, of course, we will need to go beyond reinforcement and examine other important topics such as motivation and social pressure. For the moment, though, we consider only the subject of rewards.

From observations made with rats, pigeons, monkeys, and other organisms—and some studies with humans—we have come to know a great deal about how reinforcement hooks people and gets them to behave in certain predictable ways.

Experiments with rats are the easiest to do, and certain laws of reinforcement emerge in their simplest form in a rat study.

A typical experiment to investigate reinforcement involves a white laboratory rat placed in what is called a "Skinner box," named after Harvard psychologist B. F. Skinner, who invented it. A Skinner box is a cage containing a protruding lever that the rat can push and a small container into which food can be dispensed by the experimenter. When a novice rat is initially placed into the box, it wanders around, performing the sorts of behaviors that rats typically perform: exploring, sniffing, grooming. Eventually—probably out of sheer boredom—it presses the lever, whereupon a rat pellet appears in the container. This is a reinforcing event, which undoubtedly makes the rat very happy. The event, like any reinforcement, leads to an increase in the behavior that just preceded it—in this case, lever-pressing. Eventually the rat will be pressing the lever at a rapid clip and eating rat pellets to its heart's content. Already you may be sensing a correspondence between the rat in the Skinner box and the human in front of the "video parlor box." Both are continually performing actions that lead to reinforcement. The rat gets crunchy food, while the video game player gets higher scores and free games. While food would be reinforcing for the video gamer, there are undoubtedly times when given the choice between (1) a slice of pizza and (2) a chance to play Space Invaders and perhaps achieve the high score for the day, the game would be a more powerful reinforcer.

SCHEDULES OF REINFORCEMENT

Game designers confront many decisions when trying to create a game that people will like. One question is: How often should a player be reinforced? Is it a good idea to make sure that players never leave their first game without some form of reinforcement? Or should the games be created so that they are sufficiently difficult and several plays are necessary before a single rewarding event occurs? As we shall see, game designers have apparently stumbled on the optimal strategy for reinforcing people so they (like the rat that keeps pressing) will continue dropping quarters at a rapid clip.

To see this, let's return to the rat. In the scenario we have just sketched, the rat was reinforced after each lever press. This is called continuous reinforcement—the rat gets a reward each time it presses the lever. This schedule is usually necessary to get the rat started.

However, continuous reinforcement is just one of many possible schedules of reinforcement. Suppose that after the rat starts pressing away, we stop providing food pellets after each press and instead provide them only now and then. What will the rat do? It will continue pressing, at least for a while. At some point, however, the rat will again be reinforced, since eventually another pellet will follow a lever press. This schedule of reinforcement is called partial reinforcement—reinforcement is intermittent rather than continuous. Partial reinforcement is a powerful way of hooking both rats and people. They keep responding in the absence of reinforcement because they are hoping that another reward is just around the corner. The gambler keeps pulling the slot machine lever even though he has lost ten times in a row because he hopes that the next time around he'll win big. This would never happen if reinforcement had been continuous. If it were, then as soon as the money stopped, the gambler would quickly decide that the machine was no good anymore and turn his attention elsewhere.

EXTINCTION

We knew a woman we'll call Ruth who went to Las Vegas at least twice a month. Each time she stayed for three days and spent most of her waking hours diligently pumping nickels into a slot machine. If you happened to wake up as the sun was rising, you'd find Ruth glued to the machines. Her case was classic. When she was in her early twenties, Ruth went to Las Vegas for the first time to celebrate her best friend's twenty-first birthday. While there, she experienced a "big win" of $850, which was more than her monthly salary. This experience made a lasting impression on her and from then on she was hooked.

What if reinforcement were cut off altogether? As you might expect, Ruth and the other players would not stop playing immediately. Rather, they would doggedly continue to play for some time before giving up in exasperation. This decline and eventual cessation of behavior (lever pumping) in the absence of reinforcement (money) is referred to as extinction, and the length of time it takes for the behavior to cease, or extinguish, is referred to as the extinction period.

How long will it take Ruth to stop playing these machines? This depends heavily on the schedule of reinforcement that she had been exposed to earlier. If Ruth was used to winning each time she dropped a coin, then she would extinguish very quickly. However, this continuous schedule of reinforcement would have been very unlikely in Vegas. It is far more likely that she had been reinforced intermittently—that she had been on a partial reinforcement schedule—and in this case the extinction period is considerably longer.

But which partial reinforcement schedule leads to the longest extinction periods? It turns out that the "variable" schedules (either variable ratio—say, one in five turns, on the average—or variable interval—say, every minute, on the average) are the most powerful ones because they lead to the longest extinction periods. More precisely, a variable schedule with moderately long intervals between reinforcements is a good idea for game designers since it leads people to continue to play the longest in the face of nonreward. However, if the variable schedule is *too* long, a person might actually extinguish when the game designer had not meant this to happen. With a very long interval between reinforcements, the person has no way of being sure that the reinforcement drought is ever going to end. He or she may actually give up playing rather than drop the next quarter that would lead to a reward.

In sum, we know a great deal about reinforcement and how it affects people. A partial reinforcement schedule leads to behavior that (1) occurs more rapidly and (2) is more resilient to extinction than does a continuous reinforcement schedule. The dependence of extinction on the prior schedule of reinforcement has been dubbed the partial reinforcement effect. Taken together, these two effects of partial reinforcement produce what looks very much like "addictive behavior."

The question of why the partial reinforcement effect occurs has long been of interest to psychologists, and a variety of experiments have been carried out to test various theories. For our purposes, however, the important thing is that the phenomenon happens at all. Knowing how rates of responding and resilience to extinction are affected by reinforcement schedules should—in principle, anyway—allow us to account for the seemingly addictive behavior engendered by video games. Furthermore, we can explain why some video games are more addictive than others.

With these concepts in hand, it is easy to see the underlying principle that governs behavior not only in the case of Ruth, the compulsive gambler, but also in the case of the young, aspiring astronomer and the teenager in the video parlor. In all cases, the person is under a partial reinforcement schedule: slot-machine payoffs occur only infrequently, as do shooting stars and video game wins. Moreover, the schedules are of the variable sort (slot-machine payoffs, shooting stars, and video game wins do not occur in a fixed, systematic way) and therefore produce the most powerful resistance to extinction. According to the principles of partial reinforcement, therefore, the behaviors involved should be highly resistant to extinction, which indeed they are. In all cases, the person is willing to pursue the behavior for lengthy periods of time, even in the absence of reinforcement.

REINFORCEMENT AND VIDEO GAME DESIGN

Given an understanding of these principles, the task of a person who designs and manufactures video games is more focused. The designer's goal, of course, is to make money on the game. This goal is achieved by ensuring that the eventual players will insert quarters into the game as rapidly as possible. It's to the designer's advantage to design a game that reinforces the player on the most addictive schedule possible. And this usually turns out to be a variable-ratio or a variable-interval schedule.

What this means in the world of video games is that reinforcement will be somewhat unpredictable. A reward might come on the average of once every ten times a player plays. For example, the player might achieve three complete boards in Pac-Man only once every ten times, or so, that he or she plays. This is an example of a variable-ratio schedule. If a reinforcement came on average once every ten minutes, with the actual times ranging randomly from once every ten seconds to once every half hour, our player would be on a variable-interval schedule. So, for example, if the Space Invader's mother ship appeared and was destroyed on this sort of schedule, we would say that the player was on a variable-interval schedule. These irregular schedules of reinforcement are, in part, what cause video games to be so compelling and irresistible.

In trying to implement these reinforcement schedules, an interesting problem arises for the video game designer. To understand the nature of this problem, it is useful to consider not a video game but, rather, pinball. As you probably know, pinball is played with a steel ball, initially ejected via a spring mechanism, into the playing area. While in the playing area, the ball can strike various knobs, springs, and other assorted paraphernalia, all of which cause the score to increase. If, however, the ball rolls down to where it originated, that ball is eliminated and a new ball must be ejected. The player has three kinds of control over what is going on. First, the initial ejection of the ball can range from soft to powerful, depending on how far back the player draws the spring-loaded plunger. Second, near the player is a small gate, partially guarded by flippers that the player can manipulate. These flippers, if used properly, eject the ball back into the field before it can roll out of play. And finally, the player, by using his or her whole body, can tilt the entire machine ever so slightly, in order to influence the path of the ball. The tilt can't be too much, however, or "tilt" will register on the scoreboard and the game will end.

Any game—pinball included—can't be too easy, or it will provide continuous reinforcement for practiced players, which, as we've seen, doesn't really lead to much of an addiction to the game. On the other hand, the game can't be too difficult —that is, reinforcement can't be too intermittent—because then most novice players will never get enough reinforcement to become addicted to the game in the first place. Just as the rat in the Skinner box never really begins pressing the lever unless initial reinforcement is more or less continuous, so the would-be game addict needs some early reinforcement in order to get interested in the game. This means the pinball game designer is forced to an intermediate stance—the game is made moderately difficult. This solution has two difficulties. First, and probably most serious, many potential players won't ever start playing pinball, because they don't get reinforced enough when they first start playing and can't play very well. Second, a really expert player will be reinforced continuously, which, as we've seen, doesn't produce much addiction. A colleague of ours named Graham, who teaches at the University of Aberdeen, tried a game one evening and got a score of zero. He said he never wanted to play again. A half hour later, another player —fifteen-year-old Dennis—tried the same game and, much to Graham's dismay, gave up after ten minutes because it was "much too easy."

Enter video games. The feature that sets them apart from all other games is the extremely flexible nature of the digital computer that controls them. We'll talk more about computers in chapter 6. For now, it's sufficient to realize that the computer can be programmed to make the games easy to begin with and progressively more difficult. A good example of this is seen in Pac-Man. The major determinants of difficulty in that game are such things as the speed of Pac-Man himself, the speed of the monsters, the period of time that the monsters remain edible by Pac-Man, and so on. These factors change from board to board such that the game becomes progressively more difficult as play continues. A novice player is usually able to get through one complete board after only a few trys. However, only a very few experts—who have played literally thousands of games—are able to make it up to the highest level of difficulty. The same sort of strategy is seen in the design of other popular games such as Space Invaders, where the invaders move faster, shelters disappear, and the player's life becomes generally more difficult and harrowing as the game progresses.

There is another advantage of having the computer control the reinforcement schedules. Suppose we turn into a nation of Pac-Man experts. Suppose, that is, virtually everyone practiced

Pac-Man enough to be able to play it perfectly. Wouldn't reinforcement then become continuous, with the resultant lack of addiction? No problem. Another salient feature of a computer program is that it is very easy to modify. It would be a trivial job to make the monsters go even faster or make Pac-Man go even slower. Less trivial, but still not especially difficult, would be the insertion of features that are altogether new —for example, a new monster could be created that is even more adept at devouring Pac-Man and generally creating havoc than are the current ones. In contrast, the capability of easily changing the rules of the game is not present with a precomputer game such as pinball, where all such changes would involve difficult-to-modify mechanical devices rather than simple-to-modify computer programs.

Other Aspects of Reinforcement

Knowing about the partial reinforcement effect gives any video game designer an edge in designing a particularly appealing game. But there is more that the designer needs to know. For example, Pac-Man gobbles yellow dots that are worth 10 points each. Why 10 points? Is this the best number of points to award a player for each dot devoured? These questions raise the important issue of how big the reward ought to be. Another principle of reinforcement is necessary for understanding behavior, and that concerns the size, or magnitude, of reinforcement.

MAGNITUDE OF REINFORCEMENT

There is no question that behavior is related to the size of the reinforcing event. Rats, for example, will run faster and more frequently if they are rewarded with more food rather than less food. People will work harder and play longer on a slot machine if they have a chance of winning $1,000 than if they have a chance of winning only $100. Intuitively, of course, this doesn't seem surprising.

When it comes to video games, however, the issue of reinforcement magnitude becomes a bit more interesting. You may have noticed that the number of points one accumulates in video games always seems to be very large, even if the player is just a novice. For example, in Pac-Man, a player acquires 10 points for devouring each dot, 200 to 1,600 points for devouring the monsters, and so on. Thus even on a very first Pac-Man effort, a player can generally score in excess of a few hundred points.

Why is this? Why not, for example, just one point per dot and 20 to 160 points for the monsters? At the very least, there'd be less space needed on the screen to display the score. When we look at things in terms of reinforcement principles, the reason is clear: large rewards lead to faster responding and greater resistance to extinction—in short, to more addiction—than do smaller rewards. From the point of view of the video game manufacturer, of course, points are free—the cost of manufacturing and programming the game is the same whether small or large numbers of points are awarded to the game's eventual players.

Given these considerations, you might ask why the game designers stopped where they did in terms of point magnitudes. Why only 10 points per dot in Pac-Man? Why not 100 or 1,000? The answer is twofold. First, the point magnitudes, after all, have to be something, and whatever they're made to be they could always be higher. So the actual values chosen by the designer are somewhat arbitrary. Second, however, at some point people stop having an intuitive grasp of what some magnitude means—that is, above some magnitude, any amount is psychologically pretty much equal to any other similarly high amount. To get a feeling for this phenomenon, imagine that you are a participant in a TV game show and you are given the following choice: (1) you can either have $1 for sure, or (2) a coin will be tossed, and you will receive $10 if the coin comes up heads but nothing if the coin comes up tails. Almost invariably people choose the latter alternative, figuring that $10 is worth so much more than $1 that the chance of winning the $10 is worth the risk of losing the coin toss and forsaking everything. But now imagine a new version of the choice: either you get a sure $1 million or a coin is tossed and you get $10 million if the coin comes up heads but nothing if the coin comes up tails. Now we find that people almost invariably choose the first alternative. For most people, $1 million and $10 million are psychologically pretty much the same thing—they're both "very large amounts of money." Thus it makes perfect sense, psychologically, to opt for the sure thing—the million dollars—rather than the choice that involves a 50 percent chance of getting nothing.

Bearing this example in mind, we see why video game scores —despite principles of reinforcement—can't be too large. In Pac-Man, for example, the designer wants the accomplishment of eating a monster to be psychologically much greater than the accomplishment of eating a dot. This is done by awarding differential numbers of points, but, as in the money example, the absolute value of the points can't be too large. A million points for eating a dot would, psychologically, be not very dissimilar from 20 million points for eating a monster; they are both just "huge numbers of points."

DELAY OF REINFORCEMENT

We have pointed out that any behavior will increase in frequency if that behavior is followed by reinforcement. It turns out that the delay between the behavior and the reinforcement is, in most cases, very important: the shorter the delay, the quicker will the behavior increase in frequency. In other words, short delays lead to more powerful reinforcement effects.

In many real-life situations, delay of reinforcement is very long. For example, if we save money in a savings account, it's a long time before we begin to see the interest accumulate or are able to withdraw the saved money in order to make some large purchase. Because of this delay of reinforcement, the behavior of saving money isn't as frequent as it otherwise would be—in everyday language, we say that saving money is difficult. So, many people don't save money; instead they spend it as soon as they get it, and reinforcement is immediate.

In the case of video games, however, at least some sort of reinforcement is always provided immediately. In most cases, a score of some sort is prominently posted somewhere in the display, and the score changes the instant we shoot down an enemy ship or eat a monster. It is, in part, this instant reinforcement that makes the behavior of playing video games so satisfying and therefore so prevalent.

MULTIPLE REINFORCEMENTS

One aspect of video games that sets them apart from most other games is that they can be, and usually are, much more complicated than arcade-type games have traditionally been. Pac-Man, for example, has many different ways to reinforce you. You can eat dots; you can eat monsters; you can avoid monsters; you can eat the symbols; you can get through boards; you can see between-board skits; hear music; and so on. Other games, invented more recently than Pac-Man, are even more complicated.

From the standpoint of what makes games fun, these multiple reinforcements are important because different people enjoy different things. By using a "kitchen-sink" approach— that is, by inserting into a game a wide variety of things that might be reinforcing—the designer winds up with a game that appeals to a wide variety of people and will, accordingly, be widely played. This flexibility of video games can be contrasted with that of pinball. Pinball, for all its bells and whistles, really provides only limited types of reinforcement—you see the ball move, you hear the sound effects, you see your score increasing, and that's about it. The reason for this contrast, once again, is that the computer program that underlies a video game is itself infinitely flexible, whereas pinball, being mechanical, has to be kept relatively simple or else it will become prohibitively costly.

If video games are reinforcing in a variety of ways, at least some of the reinforcement is no doubt extrinsic, taking the form of praise and admiration from peers and other onlookers. But it's perfectly possible to play a video game by yourself and feel gratified when you do well or when you improve your performance. This kind of reinforcement is called intrinsic reinforcement. Video games can provide very powerful intrinsic reinforcement, which is probably a very important reason for their success. The fundamental source of intrinsic reinforcement—the very person receiving the reinforcement—is perpetually present.

Cognitive Dissonance

As we have seen, video games have a variety of ways of reinforcing players. But, at least for the games played in video arcades, there is another side of the picture: you have to pay for them. You might expect that the reinforcement obtained from the games themselves might in some sense be countered by the punishment that stems from having to insert quarter after quarter. Interestingly enough, however, a large body of social psychological research suggests that the opposite may be true: games may be *more* reinforcing, not less, if you have to pay for them.

During the 1950s and 60s, a group of psychologists (led by Leon Festinger and his colleagues) developed a theory called cognitive dissonance to account for some seemingly paradoxical types of behavior. The paradox is that people sometimes seem to enjoy things that are less reinforcing over other things that are more reinforcing. Consider, for example, an experiment reported by Festinger and Carlsmith.[2] In this experiment, a group of people performed a repetitious, tedious, and thoroughly boring task. After completing the task, the group was asked by the experimenter to lie to a new group of people —to tell them that the task was more fun than it actually was. One group was offered $20 to lie, whereas the other group was offered only $1. Finally, after the lies had been told, the people were asked to rate how much they enjoyed the original task. It turned out that, contrary to what you might expect on the basis of reinforcement effects, the $1 group claimed to like the task much better than did the $20 group.

Why did this happen? Cognitive dissonance theory assumes that when a person performs acts or holds beliefs that are in conflict with one another, the person will act so as to reduce the conflict. In the $1/$20 experiment, the conflict was between the people's knowledge that they were performing a boring task and their knowledge that they had told someone else that the task was fun. Why did they lie? People who were

[2]L. Festinger and J. M. Carlsmith, "Cognitive Consequences of Forced Compliance," *Journal of Abnormal and Social Psychology* 58 (1959): 203–10.

paid $20 had adequate justification—they were hired guns, *paid* to lie. The $1 group didn't have this handy justification, and their only recourse was to change their attitude about the task. By believing that the task was more interesting, they created a justification for the positive report that they made about it.

We can recast this sort of finding into a statement about extrinsic versus intrinsic reinforcement. Given that a person was performing some act to begin with, it's necessary to have *some* kind of reinforcement to account for it. If there's extrinsic reinforcement, as there was for the $20 group, that's fine. But if there's insufficient extrinsic reinforcement, as was true for the $1 group, then intrinsic reinforcement had to be generated—the subjects had to decide that the task was more intrinsically fulfulling. This sort of effect can be seen more directly in an experiment by Lepper, Greene, and Nisbett.[3] Here, nursery school children were given the choice of playing or not playing with marking pens. One group of children was given a reward for playing with the pens, whereas another group was given no reward. It turned out that the reward group played with the pens *less* than did the no-reward group. Again, this appears to be the opposite of what you would expect from reinforcement theory; and again, it can be explained if you assume that, in the absence of external reward, the pens developed a powerful, intrinsically reinforcing quality of their own. As an aside, it's interesting to note that this experiment has close analogues in real life, since parents will often pay their children for academic success. This practice is probably unwise, since such extrinsic reward may remove the intrinsic

[3]M. R. Lepper, D. Greene, and R. E. Nisbett, "Undermining Children's Intrinsic Interest with Extrinsic Rewards: A Test of the Overjustification Hypothesis," *Journal of Personality and Social Psychology* 28 (1973): 129–37.

motivation that produces optimal and most satisfying academic performance.

Video games have the interesting quality that they take your money but provide you with no tangible, extrinsic rewards that you can put in your pocket and take home. By anyone's definition, having your money taken away from you is not reinforcing —on the contrary, it's punishing. This means that video games must develop qualities that provide powerful intrinsic reward. Since people are standing there having their money taken away, they must develop the attitude that whatever they're doing is a lot of fun. In other words, if games were free, people would probably like them less. To our knowledge, no research has ever been done that has appropriately compared free games with money-devouring ones in terms of how enjoyable the games are perceived to be. But a large body of psychological research indicates that games requiring at least some minimal amount of money (like a quarter) would be perceived as more enjoyable than free games.

Does this mean that arcade operators should be advised to make the games more expensive? Not necessarily. It's important to keep track of the distinction between how much a person enjoys the game on the one hand and how much the person plays the game on the other. A game that costs a dollar might be perceived as more enjoyable than a game that costs a quarter. But there comes a point at which, enjoyable or not, cost would be prohibitive and the game wouldn't be played. Thus there's a tradeoff between enjoyment and cost, which implies that some intermediate game cost is the optimal one. Any scientist would shriek in agony at this unjustifiable conclusion.

Regret and Alternative Worlds

So far we've talked about reinforcement in terms of being rewarded for things that you have done—like getting high scores. There's another side of this motivational coin, however, which is regret over things that you haven't managed to accomplish. In most situations regret is something that you just have to live with. But that's not true with video games. Often when playing a video game, the game ends because you've made a mistake, and you immediately know exactly what you've done wrong. "If only I hadn't eaten the energizer in this game before trying to grab that cherry," you say to yourself. "I *knew* it was the wrong thing to do, and I did it anyway." But now you don't have to just sit there being annoyed and frustrated. Instead you can play the game again and correct that mistake. So in goes another quarter. But in the process of playing again, you make another mistake. And spend another quarter to correct *it*. And so it goes.

Two psychologists, Daniel Kahneman and Amos Tversky,[4] have recently been studying the phenomenon of regret. To give you a flavor for the kind of things they've discovered, consider the following question:

Mr. Smith and Mr. Jones both have to catch planes. They're on different flights, but since both flights leave at 9:00 A.M., they decide to take a cab together. Owing to a combination of unfortunate circumstances, the cab is late and doesn't arrive at the airport until 9:30. On consulting with the airline agent, the two men discover that, whereas Mr. Smith's flight left on time at 9:00, Mr. Jones's flight was delayed and left at 9:28, only two minutes ago. Who is more upset, Mr. Smith or Mr. Jones?

[4]D. Kahneman and A. Tversky, "The Psychology of Preferences," *Scientific American*, January 1982: 160–73.

Given this question, people invariably and immediately report that Mr. Jones was more upset. Why is this? After all, both men missed their flights and, objectively, they're both in equal difficulty. Kahneman and Tversky offer an explanation in terms of alternative worlds that can be constructed in the mind. They propose that, when some unfortunate event occurs, the victim constructs an alternate reality in which the unfortunate event didn't occur. The less this alternative world differs from reality, the worse the victim then feels. In the example at hand, it's very easy for Mr. Jones to construct an alternative world in which he caught his flight. "If we had just gone through that yellow light instead of stopping for it," he might say to himself, "then I would have made my flight." Mr. Smith, on the other hand, would have a much more difficult time constructing an appropriate alternative world. In order for *him* to have made his flight, they would have had to have gone through the yellow light *and* have not gotten stuck behind that trailor truck, *and* have not had to wait so long for the cab to pick them up in the first place. Since Mr. Smith's alternative world would differ so substantially from the real world, he would wind up with a lot less regret than would Mr. Jones.

Regret in video game play fits quite nicely into this framework. The mistake that (in general) ends the game is the last thing, or close to the last thing, you did prior to the game ending (eating the energizer before trying to get to the other side of the maze in the example we gave before). Therefore, the alternate world in which the mistake was not made is extremely close to the real world in which the mistake *was* made—and that's just the situation that produces maximal regret. Naturally, given the opportunity to make that alternate world a reality and eliminate all your regret, you'll avail yourself of the opportunity. You play again.

An even more striking example of the alternative world

phenomenon as it operates in computer games is seen in Adventure. Adventure games are very similar to the precomputer game of Dungeons and Dragons. In them, the player is placed into some kind of hypothetical mazelike environment, where both danger and excitement abound. In one of them, for example, you (the player) are in a nuclear power plant and your mission is to find and defuse a time bomb that has been placed somewhere in the plant by a wicked saboteur. Carrying out this mission requires a complex series of actions, not the easiest of which is figuring out your way around the plant to begin with: learning not only where various rooms, nooks, and crannies are relative to one another, but also which actions—complying with the automatic security locks and so on—are necessary in order to cross from one place to another.

You actually play this game by issuing a sequence of instructions to the computer. In return, the instructions are carried out to the best of the program's ability; and, also, brief descriptions are provided of objects that can be seen and of actions that occur.

A couple of key features heighten the game's interest. First, there are lots of ways that you can go wrong and kill yourself. For instance, you can accidentally blow up the bomb, you can fall off a ledge, you can die of radiation poisoning, and so on. But fortunately, you can save the game at any stage, so if you do make a mistake, you can go back to the point at which the game had been saved—that is, prior to when the mistake had been made. Again we see a classic case of an alternative world. "If only I had put on the radiation suit," you say to yourself, "I wouldn't have died that horrible death in the radiation chamber." And since the alternative world in which you put on the radiation suit is very close to the "actual" world in which you didn't, regret is very high. But since you saved the game, you can go back and create that alternative world, thereby eliminating the regret. So you do. Computer games provide the ultimate chance to eliminate regret; all alternative worlds are available.

Research on Video Games

Since video games are a relatively new phenomenon, psychologists have, thus far anyway, performed relatively little research on the games themselves. One piece of research that has been done, however, is a Stanford University Ph.D. dissertation by Thomas Malone.[5] Malone was primarily concerned with educational techniques, and his dissertation was aimed at finding ways of making classroom learning more fun. Noting the mass appeal of video games and the intrinsic reinforcement that they provide, he ventured to suggest that these games may prove to be superb teaching devices. This educational theme recurs throughout Malone's dissertation; however, the research that he reports was concerned primarily with the features of certain games that made them fun to play.

Malone studied school children (kindergarten kids through eighth graders). All the children had been playing with computer games in a weekly class when the study began in 1979. The survey involved relatively nonstandard games, but it is still highly suggestive.

Malone asked the children to rank a variety of computer games they had played on a simple four-point scale. He then analyzed the features of the games and concluded that incorporation of a specific goal was the single most important feature in making a game enjoyable. Other popular features were score-

[5]T. W. Malone, *What Makes Things Fun to Learn? A Study of Intrinsically Motivating Computer Games* (Palo Alto, CA: Xerox, 1980).

keeping; audio and visual effects; the degree to which players had to react quickly; and randomness (unpredictable games are preferred). The games ranked highest incorporate these features; those ranked lowest don't.

Malone also asked children what they liked about the games. Almost 40 percent of the reasons the students gave dealt with fantasy. For example: "I like it because it's just like Star Wars." "I like it because it has bombs." "I like blasting holes in the other snake." Of course, children also provided other reasons. Some liked a game for its challenge, others because it was easy to do well. One student liked Petball because "you can get a high score very fast. . . . It's easy to get bonuses. I like to win; I'm a sore loser." Interestingly, while the children *talked* a lot about fantasy, the games they rated most favorably were notably low in fantasy: perhaps children are no better than adults at reporting their own motivations.

The results of Malone's survey provide interesting but inconclusive suggestions about what makes the games fun to play. His next step was to create new versions of particular games in which some of the hypothesized important features were missing. He investigated two different games, Breakout and Darts. Breakout requires primarily muscle skills, whereas Darts requires primarily thinking, or intellectual, skills.

Breakout is a derivative of Pong, the first video game, which was a simulation of table tennis. Figure 2.1 shows a typical screen display in Breakout. In this game, the player manipulates a knob that controls the vertical motion of the paddle, shown on the left side of the screen. The paddle is used to hit a ball that bounces against the wall on the right-hand side of the screen. The wall is made up of multiple layers of bricks, and each time the ball strikes the wall, it knocks out one brick. The ultimate goal is to knock out all the bricks from the wall. In addition, however, points are awarded for each brick that is knocked out, and the score is continuously displayed on the screen. The player is allowed a total of three balls and uses up one ball each time he misses the ball with the paddle.

Based on the results of his survey, Malone generated a list of features that, he hypothesized, contributed to Breakout's popularity. There are clear goals: increasing the score by knocking out bricks and ultimately tearing down the whole wall. The game keeps score. It has audio effects—tones sound when the ball bounces off a wall—and visual effects—the ball moves, the bricks break from the wall. It has fantasy—the player destroys the wall, perhaps imagining himself escaping from prison or rescuing a hostage.

Malone then proceeded to create several versions of Breakout and to compare them with the original. To see how important was the challenge of getting a higher score, he created some variations in which the computer did not keep track of the score. To see how important was the visual stimulation of watching the bricks break out, he created some variations in which the bricks did not actually break away—the ball just bounced back and forth against the wall, with a point being awarded for each bounce. To answer other questions, he created other variations. Malone's subjects—who, by the way, were Stanford students this time, rather than the younger children used in his initial survey—played the various games and indicated which ones they liked and did not like.

The results were clear. The most important feature in determining how much the game was liked was the breaking out of a brick when the brick was hit by the ball. The versions in which the wall remained intact when struck by the ball were not liked nearly as well (even though the score increased just as it had before). Two other features—the computer's keeping score and the ball's bouncing off the paddle (as opposed to being simply ejected from the paddle)—were also important,

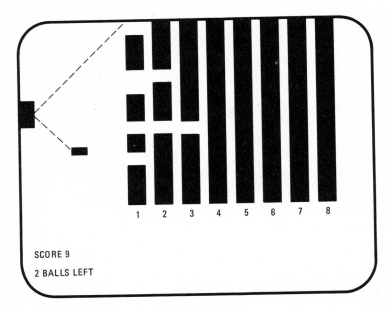

FIGURE 2.1

Breakout display. A player manipulates a knob that controls the vertical motion of the paddle shown on the very left of the screen. The paddle is used to hit a ball, which bounces against the wall on the right-hand side of the screen—a wall made up of eight layers of bricks. The score refers to the number of bricks in the wall that the player has successfully knocked out. A ball is used up whenever the player misses the ball with the paddle, and the number of balls left before the game ends is shown underneath the score.

From T. W. Malone, *What Makes Things Fun to Learn? A Study of Intrinsically Motivating Computer Games* (Palo Alto, CA: Xerox, 1980), p. 24. Used by permission of the author and the publisher. Subsequently reproduced in T. W. Malone, "Toward a Theory of Intrinsically Motivating Instruction," *Cognitive Science* 4 (Ablex, 1981): 345, and used also with permission of Ablex Publishing Co.

but less so than the gradually deteriorating wall. Why is the breaking out of the bricks so appealing? Although the experiment doesn't permit a definite answer, there are various possibilities. Watching a deteriorating wall of bricks provides visually compelling entertainment, it provides a cumulative scorekeeping device, and it shows you how far you are from reaching the ultimate goal of destroying the wall. Any one or a combination of these effects could be responsible.

Malone showed clearly that when both the score and the brick destruction were removed from the game, people didn't like it at all. Without these features, the game had very little purpose. In this degenerate version of Breakout, the players might try to keep the ball moving as long as possible but they have no easy way of knowing how well they are doing. Without the goal the game is no fun.

In Breakout, people learn a sensorimotor skill—they learn how to move the paddle in such a way as to successfully maneuver the ball. But playing Breakout doesn't require any higher-level skills such as thinking, remembering, or problem solving. For this reason, Malone next turned his attention to a new game—Darts—that did teach a bona fide academic skill, that of estimating magnitudes on a number line and expressing them as mixed numbers. (A mixed number is an integer plus a fraction, such as 1 3/8.) This experiment (in which fifth graders were used as subjects) revealed, among other things, some intriguing differences between the types of games preferred by boys and girls.

In the game of Darts, a number line is presented with specified numbers defining the ends of the line, as shown in figure 2.2. There are three "balloons" protruding from the line, and the player's job is to decide which numbers correspond to the positions of the balloons. The player types a guess, and a dart (shown on the right) is moved to the position indicated by the player and fired. If the number corresponds to a balloon's position on the line, the balloon is burst. In the example shown in figure 2.2, if the player were to type 3 3/16, the lowest balloon would burst. If the number doesn't correspond to a balloon's position, the dart remains stuck in the line and the incorrect number that had been typed in is indicated, as shown in figure 2.2. Here the player incorrectly typed 3 7/8. A total of three darts is provided; thus a perfect player can burst all three balloons.

In addition to the obvious visual effects, there are abundant auditory effects in this game. For example, circus music begins the game, and to reward the player who pops all three balloons a short song is played.

Malone again tried to find out what it was about the game that made it fun and whether any new variations would make it more enjoyable. He created a version in which, after each incorrect try, the player was told in which direction and by how much the answer was wrong. In other words, the player was given "constructive feedback" such as being told "A little too high" or "Way too low." In other variations, the balloons were broken, but not by the darts; rather, when the correct position was typed in, a balloon over on the right side of the display burst. Thus the visual display of bursting balloons was more or less the same in the two versions; however, in one the player could fantasize that the dart itself was bursting the balloon, whereas this fantasy wasn't possible in the other version. Finally, some versions of the game had the original music, whereas other versions had no music. Different players played the different versions of the game and then indicated how much they liked it.

The most intriguing result to emerge from the experiment was that boys and girls differed substantially in terms of which features determined their preferences. For every feature that

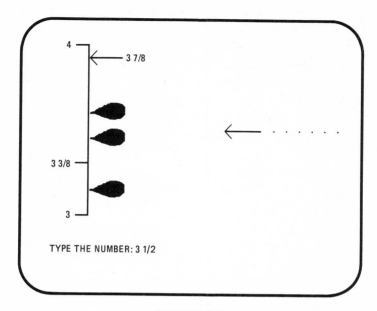

FIGURE 2.2

Darts display. Thomas Malone describes the set-up this way: "Three balloons appear at random places on a number line on the screen, and players try to guess the positions of the balloons. They guess by typing in mixed numbers (whole numbers and/or fractions), and after each guess an arrow shoots across the screen to the position specified. If the guess is right, the arrow pops the balloon. If wrong, the arrow remains on the screen, and the player gets to keep shooting until all the balloons are popped" (p. 31). In this example, the player has previously made an incorrect guess that 3 7/8 is the position of a balloon. But he's right this time by typing in 3 1/2, and the dart will move across the screen to that position, bursting the middle balloon.

From T. W. Malone, *What Makes Things Fun to Learn? A Study of Intrinsically Motivating Computer Games* (Palo Alto, CA: Xerox, 1980), p. 32. Used by permission of the author and the publisher. Subsequently reproduced in T. W. Malone, "Toward a Theory of Intrinsically Motivating Instruction," *Cognitive Science* 4 (Ablex, 1981): 349, and used also with permission of Ablex Publishing Co.

was examined, girls and boys reacted in the opposite direction —if boys liked a particular feature, girls disliked it, and vice versa. Some of the most striking differences were the following: Girls liked music, whereas boys disliked it. Girls liked (and boys disliked) being *told* (verbally) how they were doing, whereas boys liked (and girls were relatively indifferent to) having a visual, or graphic, representation of how they were doing. Finally, boys liked having bursting balloons and especially liked the version in which the balloons appeared to be burst directly by the darts. Girls disliked both of these balloon representations, and especially the latter.

In addition to these game characteristics, Malone also found that certain characteristics of the group he studied influenced how well the students liked the game. For example, those students who considered themselves to be good in math liked the game better than those who considered themselves to be poor in math. Students who thought they did well in the game liked it better than those who thought they did poorly in the game—although preference was unrelated to how well students *actually* did, providing further evidence for a distinction between what students think and what they do.

Malone worried that in reporting his results he risked perpetuating stereotypes of human beings based upon their gender. There is ample reason to believe, he urged, that the game preferences primarily reflect differences in the ways boys and girls are socialized in our culture. But whatever the basis for these preferences, it is important to understand them. For example, if a mathematical game like Darts happens to be designed in a way that appeals more to boys than to girls, then a sex difference toward mathematics may be unwittingly created.

The boys in this study liked the arrows and balloons fantasy, while the girls did not. Why? One possibility is that destroying balloons with arrows is aggressive, and the aggressiveness underlies the difference in preference.

A major reason given for why video games are fun is that they are responsive. In a world in which people are often too wrapped up in themselves to give you the time of day, the games are just the opposite. As a player, you get feedback all the time. The experiment with Darts showed that fantasy was more important than feedback, but as Malone has pointed out, the fantasy in these games is a unique form of responsive fantasy. The fantasy is feedback.

When we watch a movie or read a book, we passively observe the fantasies. When we play a computer game, we actively participate in the fantasy world created by the game. For this reason alone, the computer game might an ideal vehicle for learning. We'll return to this educational theme in chapter 5, but for the moment, it's worth noting that Malone felt he had the beginnings of a learning theory that was "intrinsically motivating." By this, he meant a kind of learning in which reinforcement comes from within the person rather than from the outside world. For Malone, there are three major ingredients inherent in the student-computer game experience that make the games such ideal vehicles for learning. These three ingredients are: challenge, fantasy, and curiosity.

Challenge comes into play because the games provide a goal to be reached and an uncertain outcome. The ideal game, if it is to provide the challenge necessary for true intrinsic motivation, undoubtedly includes an element of chance—or at least something that seems like chance to the learner. In card games, the cards are typically dealt randomly to players, and uncertainty is thereby introduced. Similarly, in a game like Darts the particular problem to be solved at any moment, whether it is the location of 3 1/2 or 2 5/8, is more or less randomly determined. Challenge is also achieved by having a "variable difficulty level": as the player gets better at the game, the game gets harder. The effort, skill, or knowledge required to reach some subgoal may increase. This keeps the player from getting bored, providing the requisite challenge.

Fantasies are the second ingredient for making a learning environment more interesting and more educational. For Malone, fantasy-inducing environments are those that evoke mental images—images of physical objects such as balloons or images of social situations such as being the ruler of a kingdom. Long before Malone's work, theorists such as child psychologist Jean Piaget assigned a central role to make-believe play in the development of skills in children. So Malone's idea about the importance of fantasy is not completely new; his contribution, rather, is to identify the important role it plays in making video games an ideal vehicle for learning.

The final ingredient for making a learning environment more interesting is the evocation of the learner's curiosity. For this, one needs to provide an optimal level of informational complexity. By optimal level, Malone means that the environment should be neither too complicated nor too simple with respect to how much the learner already knows. The world of learning should be novel and surprising; at the same time, it cannot be incomprehensible. Finding the optimally complex environment constitutes the fundamental challenge for the designers of the educational video games of tomorrow.

CHAPTER 3

GAMES AND THE COGNITIVE SYSTEM

Ability is the focus of this chapter. What aspects of mind figure in the performance of an act requiring complex skills, such as playing video games? Psychologists refer to the mind as the "cognitive system" because the "mind" isn't really a unitary entity. Rather it is an elegant system of delicately intertwined and finely tuned components. The means by which these components are combined into an ability—such as the ability to play a video game—is called a strategy. In the pages to come, we'll describe both the components themselves and the ways in which they can be combined into strategies.

A major theme of the chapter is that quite different strategies can be used for accomplishing the same mental goal—the goal, for example, of being good at a particular video game. Which strategy is appropriate for a particular person depends on which of his or her mental components are good. Some people have very fast reaction times, while others are good at memorizing things.

A second, related theme is that of time and how long it takes to do things. A typical person has a reaction time of about a fifth of a second. We'll see that the quality of many mental components is measured in terms of the amount of time that a component takes to do something. Most video games are designed so that if you're faster than the game at something, you win; if you're slower, you lose.

We have referred to the cognitive "system" and its "components." To illustrate these concepts, we'll use a familiar example: a stereo system. A sophisticated system might consist of a turntable/cartridge; amplifier; tuner; reel-to-reel and cassette tape deck; several pairs of speakers, any combination of which can be in operation at any given time; and two sets of stereo headphones. To evaluate the system, we would have to consider the quality of each component and then the degree to which the user is adept at combining the components to make the system capable of carrying out a variety of functions— producing music for a party, providing a soothing background, masking the sound of outside traffic, making tapes for the car stereo, and so forth. Since the system is so complex, it's capable of doing each of these things in a variety of ways. It's the user's job to figure out which is the best way for any given task and to configure the system accordingly.

The Mind as a System

The cognitive system, too, can be conceptualized as consisting of components, and a particular combination of these mental components, designed to accomplish some particular goal, is referred to as a strategy. Later we shall discuss how specific strategies are appropriate for specific people playing specific video games. But first, let us introduce the mental components themselves.[1]

SENSORY MEMORY

At any given moment, our five senses are being bombarded by a tremendous amount of incoming information from the environment. When, for example, you're standing in a video game parlor playing Donkey Kong, visual information originating from the game screen, as well as from much of the rest of the video parlor, is entering the cognitive system via your eyes. Auditory information in the form of honks and beeps from your game and others, along with the cries, whispers, and conversation of the denizens of the parlor, is entering the cognitive system through your ears. You're receiving tactile information from the feel of the buttons and levers of the game through the skin of your fingers, olfactory information about the hot dog being consumed by the person standing next to you, and gustatory information about the soft drink that you're sipping in between button pushes.

All information that enters the system through the sense organs is initially placed into a sensory memory. One sensory memory corresponds to each sensory modality, thus there are five sensory memories in all. Each sensory memory has a very large capacity for holding information—indeed, experimental evidence suggests that a sensory memory may hold *all* the information that initially enters the system from the environment. But information in it doesn't stay around very long. In the case of the visual modality, for example, information remains in the sensory buffer for only about a quarter of a second

[1]For a more complete description, see G. R. Loftus and E. F. Loftus, *Human Memory* (Hillsdale, NJ: Lawrence Erlbaum, 1976).

(or 250 milliseconds). Within this short time it is transferred to the next storage area of the cognitive system or decays away and is lost forever.

ATTENTION

If, as in our example, you were at the video parlor playing Donkey Kong, you would need some but by no means all of the information entering the system through your eyes, only a very small amount of the information entering through your ears and skin, and probably none of the information entering through your nose or tongue. Not only do you not need this excess information, but it you were to hold onto it, it would probably hinder you in your attempt to play the game efficiently.

However, some portion of the incoming information is critical for you. You have to be able to see what barrels are rolling toward you, for example, or you're most certainly going to be hit by them. So the question is: How do we filter out the information we don't need, while at the same time retaining the information that we do need?

This filtering process is what is referred to as attention (or selective attention), and people generally filter information very efficiently. Psychologists have shown this efficiency in studies of the "cocktail party phenomenon."[2] Imagine that you're sitting on a couch at a crowded cocktail party in which a number of conversations are occurring simultaneously. Bill and Jim are talking on your left and, at the same time, Sue and Jane are talking on your right. If you attend to Bill and Jim's conversation, then you'll find that you're completely unaware of Sue and Jane's conversation. However, it's perfectly possible to *switch* your attention to the right-hand conversation, at

[2]D. Norman, *Memory and Attention* (New York: Wiley, 1969); U. Neisser, *Cognitive Psychology* (New York: Appleton-Century-Crofts, 1967).

which point you'll stop being aware of the left-hand conversation. This switch of attention doesn't require moving a muscle —it is something that occurs completely within your mind. All the conversations from the entire party, including the two in question, have been entering your sensory memory, but you have been attending to, and thus have been aware of, only one conversation at any given time. All the others have been eliminated—filtered out of sensory memory and quickly lost from the cognitive system.

The cocktail party example involved sound—information coming in through the auditory modality. There are analogous instances of such attentional effects in the visual modality. Suppose, for example, that you're playing the game of Sabotage. Sabotage works as follows: you, the player, are in charge of a large cannon that sits on the ground. As the game progresses, you're attacked by a variety of flying objects, chiefly helicopters, and paratroopers that are dropped by the helicopters. You can use your cannon to shoot down both the helicopters and the paratroopers. You are charged one point per shot, but you earn various numbers of points for everything that you shoot down. More points are awarded for destroying helicopters than for destroying paratroopers. However, if four paratroopers manage to land unscathed, they will team up to sabotage you, thereby resulting in the destruction of your cannon and the termination of the game.

In this game you tend to concentrate on destroying helicopters until a disturbing number of paratroopers are in the air, at which point you concentrate on the paratroopers. Thus you attend to different sets of incoming information. While attending to the helicopters, for example, you're quite unaware of the paratroopers—indeed, you have to periodically shift attention away from the helicopters just to make sure that no paratroopers have slipped in unnoticed. Likewise, while concentrating on shooting down the paratroopers, you almost completely lose track of the helicopters. Again we see that all environmental stimuli—both the helicopters and the paratroopers—are perpetually registered by the cognitive system in the sense that they all enter the sensory memory.[3] However, your attentional abilities allow you to attend to only one set of stimuli or the other.

Since performance in video games depends, in large part, on the speed at which you're able to do things, the question of how fast you can shift your attention from one set of information to another is quite important. In Sabotage, for example, if you waited too long to notice the paratroopers, your game would quickly be over.

Some shifts of attention involve eye movements. What are eye movements? An explanation requires a short digression here. The entire area that we can see at all is called the total visual field. The area that's directly in the center of the visual field is called the central field and the rest is called the visual periphery.

Because of the way our eyes are built, there's much of the visual field that we can't see very well at any given instant. Rather, we can make out only fine details in the central field, which is quite small—less than 1 percent of the total visual field. To demonstrate this, try focusing your eyes on one word of text in this book. If you keep your eyes steady, you'll find that only about one word is really readable. Words on either side of the one you're focusing on—as well as words above and below it—are fuzzy and indistinct.

What about the periphery? We can see objects in the visual

___

[3]Naturally, a good deal of additional visual information is entering your sensory memory as well. For example, if you are playing this game in a video arcade, you will also be seeing other players, other games, and so on. Typically a good player is able to focus attention in such a manner that only the information corresponding to his or her particular screen is being attended to.

periphery, but we can't see them very well. Nonetheless, the visual periphery is very useful. For instance, we're able to detect when something new appears in the periphery, or when something moves or changes color. Detection of such changes in the periphery is often a sign that something interesting or important is happening there. Some event in the visual periphery often signifies that you should shift your gaze to the area where the event is occurring, in order to assess what's happening. Thus we need to make eye movements in order to keep ourselves updated on what's happening in the world. When playing Sabotage, a quick eye movement to that fuzzy object in the periphery can tell you that a bomber is on its way and that immediate action is necessary.

Not all eye movements are alike. One common type is called a saccade (French for "jerk" or "jolt") which is a quick jump of the eye from one place to another. In between saccades are periods during which the eye is relatively stationary; these are called fixations. It is during these fixations that information gets into the mind; nothing gets in while the eye is making a saccade.[4] When doing something like video game playing, where things are happening at a rapid clip, making saccadic eye movements turns out to be time-consuming. Saccades themselves take place quite rapidly—most take less than a thirtieth of a second to complete. But a bottleneck arises because once the eye arrives somewhere, it is forced to stay there for a minimum of about a fifth of a second before it can move again. That is, fixations last a minimum of about 200 milliseconds.

---

[4]It is easy to demonstrate that we see only during fixation periods. Tell a friend to look at himself in the mirror and shift his eyes back and forth so that he is looking first at one eye, then at the other. If you look at his eyes, you will see them shifting back and forth. Now look in the mirror and move your own eyes back and forth. They will look stationary to you, although to your friend they will appear to be moving. The only time you can *see* your eyes is when they've stopped moving and have become stationary.

This can cause problems if, for example, you move your eye to some particular place, quickly assess what's going on there, and then notice via your peripheral vision that something else important is happening elsewhere. Because of the inherent physiology of our visual system, you're stuck where you are for about a fifth of a second before you can switch your gaze to investigate this new development. A fifth of a second may not seem like much in the grand scheme of things, but in a video game events are taking place so fast that the difference between being able to do something in, say, a tenth of a second instead of a fifth may make a big difference.

In addition to switching attention via eye movements, it's also possible to switch attention without moving our eyes if we're switching attention between things that are very close together. Again, it's easy to demonstrate this to yourself. Stare again at a word of text; don't move your eyes. Notice that you can switch attention back and forth between two adjacent letters in the word. This type of attention shift takes about a twentieth of a second (50 milliseconds) to carry out.

SHORT-TERM MEMORY

Via the practice of selective attention, only certain information from sensory memory actually gets noticed. But what actually happens to the objects that we attend to? Attended information is transferred—that is, copied from—sensory memory to a new component of the cognitive system referred to as short-term memory.

Short-term memory has several salient characteristics. First, it is generally identified with consciousness. That is, whatever we're currently aware of, or conscious of, is exactly that information currently in our short-term memory. Second, short-term memory has a relatively small capacity. In contrast to sensory memory, which appears to be of virtually unlimited capacity, short-term memory can hold only about seven items—it's large enough to hold a seven-digit telephone number, for example. We can access the contents of short-term memory very quickly —if, for example, you're holding a string of digits (such as a telephone number) in your short-term memory, you can scan through them at the rate of about thirty digits a second (roughly one digit every 33 milliseconds). We lose information from short-term memory moderately quickly; information in it will generally be forgotten after fifteen to twenty seconds. So if you had just looked up a telephone number and someone interrupted you to ask a question, the number would probably be forgotten. However, this forgetting process can be prevented by rehearsal: by repeating the contents of short-term memory over and over to ourselves, forgetting will be prevented. By rehearsing information, we can keep it in short-term memory indefinitely. Finally, short-term memory is also our "working memory." It's where information is manipulated when we plan things, figure things out, and so on. This is important, because if we're maintaining a lot of information in short-term memory via rehearsal, we'll have less short-term memory capacity left to do other things, such as planning strategies and focusing attention. Suppose that you're playing Defender. While you're playing, you have a good deal of planning to do. You have to be constantly thinking about where you'll be aiming, whether you might want to escape into hyperspace, and so on. In order to carry out all of this, it is important to have your short-term memory clear. Short-term memory is like the amplifier in the stereo system; it's the heart of the system, and it's important to learn to use it as efficiently as possible.

LONG-TERM MEMORY

The next major component of the cognitive system is long-term memory—our repository of general knowledge. It contains such things as our name, our ability to speak the language, things that we've learned at work or in school, and so on.

The storage capacity of long-term memory is virtually unlimited. Further, while information can be forgotten, such forgetting is relatively slow. Whereas information is lost from sensory memory in less than a second, and from short-term memory in less than a minute, information will remain in long-term memory for days, months, years, or even decades. How long it will remain depends on how well it was originally stored there. Since information makes its way into long-term memory via short-term memory, it's necessary to keep information in short-term memory for some period of time in order to get it into long-term memory. This makes intuitive sense. If you're told a person's name and don't attend to it at all—or even if you attend to it but then immediately forget it—you'll be unable to remember the name later on.

In general, you'll find that if you just maintain information in short-term memory by rehearsing it, then the longer you maintain it, the better it will be entered into long-term memory. The efficiency of entering information into long-term memory can be improved by so-called elaboration methods. They include such tricks as forming mental images of whatever it is you're trying to remember, associating the to-be-remembered information to things that you already know, or making up rhymes such as "Thirty days hath September . . ."

When you learn a new video game, you have to remember many things about how to play the game and what the consequences are of various actions. Under what circumstances is it useful to turn tail and run instead of taking an offensive stance? How long will your armored shield last before becoming useless? How many points does it cost you for each shot? And so on.

In playing video games, speed is of the essence—particularly the speed with which you can *retrieve* information from long-term memory. Psychological experiments have revealed that when you're confronted with a very familiar symbol, such as a letter, it takes you about a tenth of a second to retrieve, or to recognize, the name of that symbol.[5] This fact is important in a game such as Asteroids, in which various types of objects (for example, large asteroids, small asteroids, UFOs, and so on) appear at random times and in random places, and it's your job to identify them as soon as possible so you can take appropriate action. Since it takes about a tenth of a second to determine what each one is, a limit is placed on how fast you can deal with these objects as they appear. A game designer could thwart the efforts of most people to play a game by designing the game so that players are required to recognize objects in only a twentieth of a second.

When you sit down to play a new video game, you will find that the games you played earlier in the day can influence how well you do on the new game. The earlier games can actually interfere with your ability to learn the new one. *Interference* more generally is an important characteristic of long-term memory; it refers to the problem you have remembering one thing as a result of learning some other, related thing.

Interference can work in two directions—forward and backward. So, games you learned earlier can influence a new game you are currently learning. But the game you are currently learning can also influence the ease with which you will learn future games. This is especially true if the games are similar to one another. Knowing the problems that interference can create, some choices of what games to play in succession are wiser than others.

[5]M. I. Posner and R. F. Mitchell, "Chronometric Analysis of Classification," *Psychological Review* 74 (1967): 392–409; E. Hunt, "Mechanics of Verbal Ability," *Psychological Review* 85 (1978): 109–30.

Suppose you've learned to play Asteroids and you then become intrigued with Defender, which is similar to Asteroids but also has some important differences. You may concentrate on Defender for a while and become quite good at it. However, if you then go back to playing Asteroids, you may discover that your game has deteriorated and that you're now making responses that are appropriate to Defender—the game you just learned—but not appropriate to Asteroids, the game you originally learned. Learning Defender would have created retroactive, or backward, interference with respect to playing Asteroids.

Similarly, suppose that you have learned a whole series of "shoot-'em-down" type games such as Astro Blaster, Space Invaders, Gallaxian, and so on. Now you're getting a little bored and want to learn a new game. If the new game is another shoot-'em-down type—for example, Phoenix—you'll find that it will be hard to learn; interference from the games you already know will cause inappropriate responses. This would be an instance of proactive, or forward, interference. Chances are that you would have an easier time learning an entirely new kind of game, such as Pac-Man or Donkey Kong.

One final aspect of long-term memory is pertinent to the learning of video games. You may find that when you start learning a new game, you'll play continuously for hours and hours. Not only will this tend to deplete your supply of quarters, but, it turns out, it's not the optimal way to learn. For obvious reasons, this kind of learning strategy is referred to as massed practice. Massed practice has been found to be inefficient relative to spaced practice, in which you take numerous breaks between games. You may have noticed that if you play many games in a short period of time, you eventually seem to be getting worse rather than better. Moreover, if you take a break and return the next day, let's say, then on your very first try you may do the best you've ever done. This is known as reminiscence. It's probably the most dramatic example of the advantages of spaced practice.

EXPECTANCY

Suppose the game you are playing requires you to press a button the moment you notice that an enemy saucer has materialized out of hyperspace onto your screen. This is an example of one of the most fundamental tasks the cognitive system has to do—it has to respond as soon as possible after some event occurs in the visual field. Earlier we mentioned that it takes about a fifth of a second to react to such a stimulus. However, this figure is highly dependent on the degree to which you expect the event to occur. If you're not expecting something, it takes longer to react; if you are expecting something, it takes less time to react.

When you're learning to play a video game, therefore, it's important to know as accurately as possible when things are likely to occur so that you can anticipate them and react as quickly as possible. The difference between a reaction time of a fourth of a second (250 milliseconds) and a fifth of a second (200 milliseconds) can easily be the difference between shooting down the enemy and getting shot down yourself. In any event, being able to anticipate is a matter of learning contingencies among various events. In other words, given that some particular event has occurred—say, the appearance of an enemy ship in Space Invaders—what is most likely to happen next?

In fact, a variety of things could happen next, and what *will* happen depends on the goals of the people who originally designed the game. If they wanted to make things very difficult for you, they could design things to happen completely randomly, in which case no event will be predictive of any other event and you will never be able to put expectancy to use. However, most games (and real life) do not work this way. Usually, the occurrence of a particular event provides you with information about what will happen in the immediate future: some events have an increased probability of occurring, whereas others have a decreased probability of occurring. It is an important task of long-term memory to store these event dependencies, and good players concentrate on doing just that. In other words, when learning to play a game, they concentrate on what events are likely to follow—or not to follow—what other events. This way, they are able to use this information in the future and set up appropriate expectancies for what is about to happen. The major benefit of this strategy is that these players are able to respond faster, and that is one of the major reasons that they are good players.

THE VERBAL/VISUAL DISTINCTION

The graphic designs, the funny bleeping sounds, and the brief verbal messages are some of the most enticing qualities of video games. Occasionally the mind is strained while it is forced to deal with all of this incoming information at once. Coping with visual information (such as the designs), auditory information (such as the bleeps), and verbal information (such as the messages) simultaneously can, however, be a lot easier for a person than coping with multiple visual, multiple auditory, or multiple verbal inputs at one time.

To simplify the discussion, let's consider the visual versus verbal comparison. It's fairly clear that we have two separate mental subsystems to handle these two separate types of inputs. Further, it appears that the two mechanisms can operate independent of one another. To see what we mean by this, let's return to the stereo system example. Suppose you wanted to record from a record and from a radio at the same time. You would be able to do this by recording from the record on your cassette recorder at the same time that you recorded from the radio on your reel-to-reel recorder. Like the handling of verbal and visual information by the cognitive system, these two operations could be carried out simultaneously and independently by the stereo system.

To get a feeling for the presence of both your verbal and visual subsystems, try the following demonstration. First, imagine the block letter E. Now imagine yourself going around the letter, identifying each corner as an "in" corner or an "out" corner. The speed at which you can perform this task depends very strongly on the manner in which you make the actual identification of each corner. Try it in two different ways. First, just *say* (out loud) either "in" or "out" as you mentally arrive at each corner. Now try it again, but this time, *point* to either your left or your right to signify "in" or "out." You'll find that the pointing method will take you much longer than the speaking method. It's usually a very powerful and dramatic effect.[6] Why does this effect occur? The reason is that the task of imagining the block letter and determining whether a particular corner is an in or an out corner is a visual task. Pointing is another visual task, whereas speaking is a verbal task. Thus, when you're imagining the corners and pointing at the same time, you're doing two visual tasks at the same time, which overloads the visual mechanism. However, when you're imagining the corners and speaking at the same time, you're doing one visual task and one verbal task. Your visual and verbal mechanisms don't interfere with one another; they have no trouble operating at the same time.

This independence of visual and verbal mechanisms manifests itself in a variety of ways when video games are being

[6]L. R. Brooks, "Spatial and Verbal Components of the Act of Recall," *Canadian Journal of Psychology* 22 (1968): 349–68.

played. Practiced video players are perfectly capable, for example, of holding a conversation—with colleagues, with themselves, or with the machine itself—without impairing their ability to execute the visual/motor activities needed to play the game. Such players can also execute these abilities at the same time as they are verbally working out a strategy for the seconds to come ("Let's see, I'll pick up that energizer in the upper left-hand corner, then zoom to the middle of the board for the cherry, then get all the dots in the lower right, but leave the energizer intact . . ." a player might say to herself as she deftly gobbles up the dots and avoids the monsters). However, the same player would be ill advised to imagine one path of Pac-Man—a visual activity—while at the same time engaging in the other visual activity of actually guiding Pac-Man around the maze.

From the standpoint of video game playing, one important facility that is associated with the visual subsystem is that of mental transformations. In general, a mental transformation is the process of taking some visual stimulus and imagining it to be in some physical state other than the one it's in. For example, you could look at an object in the room, such as a chair, and mentally shrink it or expand it, or place it somewhere else in the room, or rotate it to another position. To get a feeling for what a mental transformation is, suppose you are driving a car, headed south. Suppose also that you must make a complex series of turns to get where you are going and you must consult a map. But a problem arises: if you hold the map in its normal way, with north facing upward, since you are driving south, the directions on the map won't correspond to the directions in which you must go. There are two common solutions to this problem. Some people will keep rotating the map, so that "up" on the map will always be the same as the direction in which the car is traveling. Other people, however, have the ability to "mentally rotate" the map so that they can always *imagine* it as being oriented in the same direction as the car. This latter solution involves a particular kind of mental transformation known as mental rotation.

It's easy to see how an ability to perform mental rotations could help your video game playing. In Asteroids, for example, you must mentally move a target asteroid to where it's going to be in a few seconds and, at the same time, mentally rotate your cannon to see if you're going to be in the correct position to shoot it down. Likewise, when objects move off the screen, you must be able to mentally calculate where they're going to reappear if you're going to keep an edge on the game.

The map-reading example illustrates that people differ in their ability to perform mental transformations. Some people are able to rotate the map mentally, whereas others must rotate it physically in order to understand where they're going. Using an ingenious procedure developed by Roger Shepard[7] of Stanford University in which people are timed while they mentally rotate objects, it has been found that people who are good at visualizing things are faster to mentally rotate objects than are people who are poor at visualizing. Moreover, children and elderly adults are slower to mentally rotate than are middle-age adults. Men are occasionally faster than women but sometimes the sexes perform equally quickly. This observation enables us to explain why a person can perform exceptionally well on one video game but not on another. If the second game requires especially fast mental rotation and the person happens not to be an especially fast mental rotater, he or she may never be able to master it.

[7]R. N. Shepard and L. A. Cooper, *Mental Images and Their Transformations* (Cambridge, MA: MIT Press, 1982); M. Lansman, "Ability Factors and the Speed of Information Processing," in M. P. Friedman, J. P. Das, and N. O'Connor, *Intelligence and Learning* (New York: Plenum, 1981), pp. 441–57.

People also differ quite substantially in their ability to process information visually versus verbally. For example, males tend to do better than females on those spatial tasks that require the visualization or manipulation of objects in space. However, the advantage that males have over females is rather slight, and most probably arises from different learning experiences rather than from any innate sex distinction. More generally, it is clear that some individuals—regardless of their sex—do better at one thing relative to another.

We have already suggested that good visualizers have an edge in video game playing relative to poor visualizers. The reason for this, of course, is that video games, by their very nature, require visual thinking. The visually represented objects on the screen are constantly changing, and a person who is able to mentally track these changes, and who can imagine what the configuration of objects will be several seconds hence, is in a better position to plot the appropriate actions than is the person who doesn't have these abilities. We can speculate that these individual differences in proclivity to use visual versus verbal strategies are, in part anyway, what makes some people seem inherently good at playing video games whereas others seem inherently not so good.

We have already described how different strategies may be used to accomplish the same goal. The distinction between visual and verbal thinking provides an apt example of how different strategies may be put to use. As we have mentioned, most video games emphasize the use of visual skills. Where does this leave a person who isn't so good at visual thinking? Probably the best solution for playing the games is to work out novel strategies that emphasize verbal skills instead. In Pac-Man, for example, progress can be made in various ways. One way is to just rely on your instincts, judging which way the monsters and you are going to be headed and trying generally to aim Pac-Man so that he and they won't converge when they're not blue but will converge when they are. This kind of "seat of the pants" strategy basically makes use of visual skills.

But you could also use more rational, logical, verbal strategies. For example, you could memorize and plan out various routes that you have established as being relatively safe. Or you could devise an intermediate strategy of, say, planning the order in which you're going to eat the energizers and plan to avoid the monsters as best you can in between.

How do you tell whether or not you are a good visualizer? If someone looks at a watch and tells you that it is 8:37, can you easily conjure up a mental picture of a clock reading 8:37? Or do you have to struggle to mentally create this image, slowly picturing the small hand set at 8 and then, while trying to keep the small hand glued to where it belongs, picturing the large hand pointing to the lower left-hand corner? There are several psychological tests that have been used to measure how good at visualizing a person is, some of which have been used by Canadian psychologist Allan Paivio.[8] For example, in one test Paivio asked subjects to think of a cube of a certain size and color that is sliced up into many smaller cubes. Next subjects were asked how many of the smaller cubes have two colored surfaces, how many have three colored surfaces, and so on. Based on the results of this test, as well as others, subjects could be characterized as being good or poor at visualization.

There is another test that can assist you in determining whether you are a good visualizer. In Figure 3.1 you will see a list of pairs of states with their shapes shown in the right-hand column. Look only at the names on the lefthand side (covering the shapes on the right), and place the six pairs in order so that the pair whose shapes are most similar are at the top of the list and the pair that is least similar is at the bottom. Now repeat the process while looking only at the shapes.

Are your two lists similar to each other? If you put pair B (Colorado–Oregon) near the top of both lists and pair C (Oregon–West Virginia) near the bottom, you may have fairly good visual imagery. Note that this is not a good test for distinguishing exceptional visualizers, since most people looking only at the names make judgments that are fairly similar to their judgments when looking only at the shapes. One exception to this

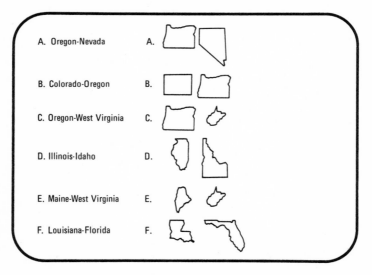

A. Oregon-Nevada
B. Colorado-Oregon
C. Oregon-West Virginia
D. Illinois-Idaho
E. Maine-West Virginia
F. Louisiana-Florida

FIGURE 3.1

How good a visualizer are you? See the text for instructions.

From M. Matlin, *Cognition* (New York: Holt, Rinehart & Winston, 1983), p. 106, based on R. N. Shepard and S. Chipman, "Second-order Isomorphism of Internal Representations: Shapes of States," *Cognitive Psychology* 1, no. 1 (1970): 1–17. Redrawn and used by permission of Holt, Rinehart & Winston, Inc., Academic Press, Inc., M. Matlin, R. N. Shepard, and S. Chipman.

consistency in judgment is Nevada; many people from the eastern United States are under the erroneous impression that most of the Western states are square, and this distorts their ability to judge the similarity of shapes when given only the names.

Tests such as these can be used to identify people who have a facility with visualization and consequently those who are likely to be good at video games that require a visualization skill.

Motor Performance

We have concentrated so far on how information is gotten from the environment and is then manipulated within the cognitive system. Operating somewhat independently of the cognitive system is the motor system, the part of the mind responsible for initiating muscle movements. The sort of skilled movement required for video games is called motor performance.

SKILL

A skill is a precise, finely tuned sequence of muscle movements, usually designed to achieve a very specific goal. In general, a skill is carried out in conjunction with feedback from the sensory system. For example, a golf pro would never have learned his or her skill without being informed where the ball landed after each stroke. Similarly, to become an expert at playing a video game, you need not only to develop the correct muscle patterns but also to coordinate the appropriate sequences with the appropriate input from the screen —that is, you need to develop what is referred to as eye-hand coordination. While playing Pac-Man, for instance, you need to be able to appropriately manipulate the joystick (a muscle skill) in a way that is dependent on such things as where Pac-Man is in the maze, where he is relative to the monsters, and so on.

PRACTICE

By any measure of performance quality that we use—time to carry out the response, correctness of the response, or whatever—performance will get better the more practice you've had. Most of the improvement occurs when you're just starting. Even if you're very poor when you begin learning a game, you'll almost certainly improve rapidly—at least at first. Then your "improvement curve" (figure 3.2) begins to flatten out: the longer you play, the slower your subsequent improvement will be. The curve is (at least roughly) logarithmic: every doubling of the number of practices leads to an equal increment in performance. Thus the second practice will produce the same improvement as the first. However, to then get the same increment again requires two more practices for a total of four. To get it yet again, you need four more for a total of eight. Then you need to double your practices to sixteen, then to thirty-two, and so on. Small wonder it is time-consuming to become a really expert player.

Actually, this logarithmic rule is pertinent to improvement in almost anything. A speaker system that costs, say, $1,000 certainly doesn't seem ten times as good as one that costs $100, because quality of the speaker system is logarithmically related to the effort of making it. You keep having to double the effort that goes into the system in order to obtain each additional unit increase in the system's quality. Since you pay according to the effort, this means that price will rise much faster than quality.

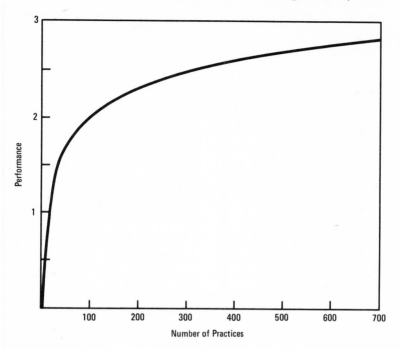

FIGURE 3.2

The improvement curve.

The amount of effort (practice) that you have to put into a skill will, by the same reasoning, increase faster than the quality of the skill. But notice another feature of this curve—it keeps going up forever. No matter how much you practice, you'll always keep getting better.

Various experiments have demonstrated this assertion. In a study completed over twenty years ago, workers in a Cuban cigar-manufacturing company who had rolled as many as 10 million cigars continued to increase their speed of rolling ci-

65

gars. However here, as in virtually all cases, the rate of improvement decreased.[9]

That we can continue to improve is a feature of the human motor system that is particularly felicitous when you are becoming skilled at a video game since, as pointed out earlier, most video games are programmed to keep getting harder and harder as you keep getting better and better.

With practice, many motor skills become increasingly automatic. You can drive a car and carry on a conversation at the same time because both of these skills are highly practiced. When a motor skill becomes automatic, it means that it can be done with a minimum of conscious control. Since conscious control is not needed anymore for completion of the motor skill, it can be used to concentrate on other features of the environment. A skilled pianist, for example, can forget about the specific motor movements and concentrate instead on interpreting the mood of a concerto, and an ace tennis player can play a decent game of tennis while carrying on a conversation. The similar "automaticity" occurs with truly experienced video gamers. We watched a skilled Pac-Man player effortlessly control the joystick while simultaneously talking with a friend and periodically reaching with her other hand to take a sip of beer. Clearly her impressive performance had reached a level of smooth, autonomous mastery.

MOTOR/COGNITIVE INDEPENDENCE

This autonomy is one consequence of an independence that develops between the cognitive and motor systems. Many years ago, one of the authors (GL) broke a finger and couldn't drive his sports car. Strapped into the passenger seat, he found him-

[9]E.R.F.W. Crossman, "A Theory of the Acquisition of Speed-Skill," *Ergonomics* 2 (1959): 153–66. Cited in D. R. Moates and G. M. Schumacher, *An Introduction to Cognitive Psychology* (Belmont, Calif.: Wadsworth, 1980).

self unable to tell the substitute driver where reverse was in the gearshift configurations. Instead he had to actually move into the driver's seat and (somewhat painfully) go through the motions of putting the car into reverse. His motor system knew perfectly well where reverse was, but his cognitive system apparently didn't have a clue. (And the motor system wasn't about to reveal the whereabouts of reverse to its cognitive colleague.) In this episode the cognitive and motor systems apparently functioned relatively independently.

When you learn a motor skill, it is not under control of the motor system from the start. At first you spend a lot of time thinking about what you're doing. As learning progresses, it gets taken over to a greater and greater degree by the motor system. This phenomenon is nicely illustrated when you learn to touch-type. After you have memorized the keyboard and fingering, you still have to take cognitive (conscious) steps of going to long-term memory to retrieve information about both the location of the key you want to strike and the finger responsible for it. Only then is the motor system summoned to perform the action. Gradually control is transferred from the cognitive to the motor system. In fact, the expert typist, unlike the beginner, is typically *unable* to quickly and accurately reproduce the keyboard any more. What the fingers have learned, the mind has forgotten.

In recent years, a pair of books entitled *Inner Tennis* and *Inner Skiing* have appeared.[10] Their major message is that, when you're trying to learn a motor skill such as tennis or skiing, it's highly detrimental to think about what you're doing. Instead you should just turn control over to the motor system and let it go. The authors of these books depict the cognitive and motor systems as two "selves," the cognitive system being

[10]W. T. Gallwey and B. Kriegel, *Inner Skiing* (New York: Random House, 1977); W. T. Gallwey, *The Inner Game of Tennis* (New York: Random House, 1974).

"Self 1" and the motor system being "Self 2." Indeed, a good strategy for something like skiing—which is almost entirely a motor skill—would be to think about something else (do arithmetic problems in your head, for example), thus disabling the cognitive system and rendering it unable to do its mischief.

MORE ON EYE-HAND COORDINATION

Eye-hand coordination is essentially the ability to perform an appropriate sequence of motor skills in response to a particular sequence of information entering the visual system from the environment. It isn't exactly that some particular pattern of muscle movements gets connected to some specific sequence of visual input. Rather, the relationship is mediated by some intervening, higher-level goal. Suppose, for example, that you are driving down a highway. Your hands are on the top of the steering wheel at the two o'clock and ten o'clock positions. The connection between visual input and motor action seems quite straightforward—if the road curves left, your hands "automatically" move left. Road right means hands right. Suppose, though, that you shift your hands to the bottom of the steering wheel—to the five o'clock and seven o'clock positions. The appropriate muscle movements for a particular visual input are now the exact opposite of what they were when your hands were on top of the wheel. Now when the road curves right, you must move your hands left, and vice versa. It's not just that you've learned two visual/motor associations, one for "hands on top of wheel" and the other for "hands on the bottom of the wheel"; you perform the appropriate muscle sequence effortlessly no matter where on the wheel your hands happen to be. Thus the appropriate connection can't be between a particular visual input and a particular muscle sequence. Rather, the connection must be between visual input, the muscle sequence, and some higher-level goal (in this case, keeping the car on the road). This is an elegant and extremely efficient—but not very well understood—manner of designing a system of eye-hand coordination.

The reliance of motor skills on higher-level goals is obviously beneficial when video games are being played because it means that once a particular skill has been learned, it will transfer to slightly different physical configurations of the same game. We knew an expert Pac-Man player, for example, who had learned the game at the video arcades. She was introduced to a home-computer version of the game in which Pac-Man was directed not by a joystick but by certain keys on the computer keyboard. It took her very little time to become just as expert at this game as she had been at the original arcade version. In this instance, the actual motor response—pressing the appropriate configuration of keys—was entirely different from the original response of manipulating the joystick. But the higher-level goals—guiding Pac-Man to the correct areas of the board, avoiding the monsters, and so on—had not changed, and it was these higher-level goals at which she had become an expert.

Strategies

So far we have been primarily concerned with each component of the cognitive system as it applies to video games. Thus we have seen how focused attention can be useful or detrimental, how various types of interference can cause deterioration of video game performance, and so on. Now we want to talk a little more about how all the components work in concert. A particular choice of which cognitive components will be used and how they will get put together is termed a strategy. Earlier we discussed how a stereo system's performance depended both on the workings of the individual components (a factor over which one has only limited control) and on strategy, how the user chooses to arrange the components. For example, if you wanted to provide a classical music background while you were working in your basement workshop, you might set the FM tuner to a classical station and switch on the speakers you've set up in the workshop. But if you wanted to fill the house with your favorite rock 'n roll music, you might use the record player rather than the tuner and use all the sets of speakers.

STRATEGIES FOR PLAYING VIDEO GAMES

There are also appropriate cognitive strategies for playing video games, from simple and obvious to complex and subtle. Consider, for example, the simple game of Breakout, in which, you will recall, there is a brick wall against which you hit a ball using a paddle. Each time the ball hits the wall, a brick disappears and you gain some number of points. Your goal is to eventually knock out all the bricks in the wall.

This game is quite simple and thus requires a fairly simple cognitive strategy. In large part, the game calls for focusing visual attention on where the ball is relative to where the paddle is. There are virtually no memory requirements. But consider, in contrast, a much more complex game such as Pac-Man. You need to focus attention on where you are, where the nearest escape route is, where the monsters are, and whether they're blue or not (recall that a blue monster can be eaten by Pac-Man rather than vice versa). You have to use your short-term memory to remember such things as what board you're on, how many Pac-Men you have left, how many energizers you've consumed, how long it's been since the monsters have been blue, and so on. You need to use your long-term memory in order to remember the configuration of the maze, where the escape tunnels are, and the behavior of the monsters in certain situations.

Given this complexity, there are various appropriate cognitive strategies. For example, you could rely primarily on long-term memory and memorize routes that work well in a variety of situations. But such a strategy would have several costs. First, you would have to memorize the strategies in the first place, which would require a lot of time (and a lot of quarters). Second, you would have to devote some of your processing capability to remembering where you are in a given route and where the appropriate place to go next is. This, of course, means less processing capability for such things as focusing and switching attention. Another disadvantage is that video game makers can easily change the routes of the monsters, thereby rendering your carefully learned routes obsolete. Finally, one wrong turn causes your route to become fouled up. A different strategy might be to forgo the specific routes and concentrate instead on trying as hard as possible to avoid the monsters, while still staying in the general vicinity of the uneaten dots. This way, use of memory would be kept to a minimum. You wouldn't care about exactly where you were in the maze at any given time. The general idea would be that if you could keep avoiding the monsters, you would eventually get all the dots. This strategy is somewhat inelegant, as you keep fussing around, apparently aimlessly, for quite some time. However, it avoids the pitfalls of the memorization strategy.

Given that there are at least two (and probably more) appropriate cognitive strategies to use, which one should you use? One expert, Ken Uston,[11] is partial to the route strategy and, in fact, devotes most of his book to describing and developing very sophisticated and complex routes. Prior to writ-

[11]K. Uston, *Mastering Pac-Man* (New York: New American Library, 1982).

ing his Pac-Man book, Uston had already achieved a good deal of fame for his development and popularization of gambling strategies, notably for the game of blackjack.[12] Like his Pac-Man strategies, his gambling strategies are based on very complex memorization strategies. Uston became an expert at these schemes and used them to make huge amounts of money in Las Vegas, Reno, and other international gambling spots. Thus it is clear that Uston, by his nature or through a great deal of practice, is an expert at memorizing and, for him, mastering a new strategy based on memorization would be natural and easy.

But if you are a poor memorizer, you might want to develop a strategy that requires a minimum of memorization. If you are slow at retrieving information from long-term memory, you'll want a strategy that minimizes such retrieval, and so on.[13]

More generally, video game players may be concerned with a "strategy for developing strategies." Most current video games are complex, requiring complex strategies. One way of combating this complexity, which actually applies to problem solving in general, is to break the required actions down into constituent parts. In figure 3.3 we have done this for the game of Sabotage. This breakdown yields a hierarchical, or treelike, structure, where points on the tree are goals and subgoals that we wish to accomplish. At the top is our overall goal of making as many points as possible. Two major subgoals are used to achieve this overall goal—keeping from being bombed and keeping paratroopers from accumulating on the ground. Each

---

[12]K. Uston and R. Rapoport, *The Big Player* (New York: Holt, Rinehart & Winston, 1977).

[13]Recall that it takes about 100 milliseconds to retrieve a name from long-term memory and bring it back into short-term memory. Actually, there is substantial variation in this figure. For example, the time tends to be lower for people with high verbal ability than for people with low verbal ability. Similarly, the time is greater with increasing age and when people are under the influence of various types of drugs.

of the subgoals is itself achieved by one or more subgoals that are nested underneath it.

When you break things down this way, it becomes much easier to see exactly what has to be accomplished. Notice also that at the bottom of the tree are relatively simple motor skills that have to be learned. Once you have identified these bottom-level goals—these specific skills—you should, if at all possi-

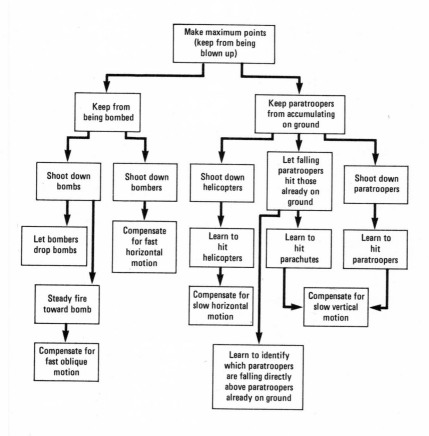

FIGURE 3.3

Sabotage: the hierarchy of its goals.

ble, practice each one in isolation since that will optimally provide you with the action/feedback sequences necessary for learning the skill.

To see the utility of using a hierarchical strategy, let us take an example of *not* using it. Recall that the predominant action in Sabotage is the appearance of helicopters that, if you don't destroy them with your gun, drop paratroopers. Helicopters (being large) are both easier to hit and worth more points than paratroopers (which are smaller). Moreover, if you concentrate on shooting down each helicopter as soon as it appears, it won't get much of a chance to drop paratroopers anyway. Thus focusing attention on helicopters and trying to hit each one as soon as it appears seems to be a reasonable strategy.

However, this strategy works only up to a certain point, because eventually helicopters start appearing and dropping paratroopers at such a frenetic pace that the sky soon becomes filled with paratroopers, and you're reduced to firing blindly and continually. Since each shot costs a point, you start losing points faster than you gain them. It's hopeless anyway, since even this desperate behavior soon becomes inadequate to catch *all* the paratroopers. So you watch helplessly as you're surrounded and eventually blown away.

The strategic error in this line of play is in not developing the subskill of shooting down paratroopers during the early phases of the game when they appear only infrequently and you can practice at a leisurely pace. Realizing this error, you would change strategies and, in the early phase of the game, deliberately allow the helicopters to survive and to drop their paratroopers. Using this gambit, you could concentrate fully on picking off the paratroopers. When you finally develop some proficiency at this skill, you can return to the strategy—overall, more efficient—of shooting down the helicopters as rapidly as possible. But at the same time, you will be secure in your knowledge that when the number of paratroopers starts to increase, you can accurately and calmly hit each one with a single shot.

Video Games as Problem Solving

Before we can master a game, we have to learn to play it. The process of moving from novice to highly proficient player can be viewed as problem solving, a process that has been studied extensively by psychologists.

There are three major aspects of a problem-solving situation: (1) the original state, (2) the goal state, and (3) the rules. For example, imagine your goal is to become proficient at Pac-Man. The original state, or the situation at the beginning of the problem-solving process, might be, "I have played games before but never a video game." The goal state, reached when the problem is solved, is to become proficient at Pac-Man. You might even make a more specific goal for yourself, such as beating the previous high score on the machine at the video parlor on Saturday, April 18. The rules refer essentially to restrictions that must be followed as you go from the original state to the goal state. They might include your wanting to become an expert on the arcade rather than the home version of Pac-Man, or to accomplish your goal without consulting any of the books on the game.

Good problem solvers seldom strike out randomly. Rather, they plan. Often they break the problem into smaller subproblems, then concentrate on solving those subproblems. In our observations of players in video parlors, we have occasionally come upon a person who sits down at a new game, inserts a quarter, and begins moving the joystick around without any idea whatsoever about the goal of the game. This approach typically gets the person nowhere.

The video player who mindlessly plunges in is failing to appreciate the importance of the first phase of problem solving —understanding the problem. To understand a problem, you must pay attention to the important aspects of it and ignore the rest. In Pac-Man, it is obviously important to pay attention to Pac-Man, the monsters, and the energizers. The elapsed time since an energizer was consumed is important. Whether the monsters are blue or not is vital. However, whether a monster happens to be green or pink is unimportant and irrelevant.

Once you, the problem solver, figure out what is essential, the next step is to try one or more different strategies for solving the problem. If your initial goal in Pac-Man is to eat all the dots on a board and win a new one, you might begin by randomly moving the joystick in one of the four possible directions. If you did this enough times, you might eventually stumble on a method for achieving your goal. However, this random approach would be inefficient and unsophisticated. A more creative approach would be to try selective routes, routes that would be more likely to lead to the goal. These selective approaches are called heuristics, and they are far more efficient than random methods. The novice Pac-Man player might try running Pac-Man around the edge of the screen and then attempting to eat the dots in the middle areas. This particular heuristic might not lead to the desired goal immediately, but it could lead to the postulation of other heuristics that might then be tried and might ultimately succeed. One problem with the "edge-then-middle" heuristic is that all of the energizers would be consumed early in the game, and none would be available later, when Pac-Man desperately needed them.

Clearly, a heuristic that does not deplete the supply of energizers is called for.

During the course of solving the Pac-Man problem, new strategies will be discovered. When the authors first started playing Pac-Man, we used to immediately consume an energizer whenever one of the four monsters was pursuing. We soon learned that it was far better to wait until the monster was close at hand before consuming the energizer. This increased our opportunity to contact and destroy the monster while still in an energized state. When learning to play a video game, good players use many heuristics of this sort.

The process of dividing a problem into a number of subproblems, or smaller problems, is called means-ends analysis and is a feature of many successful problem-solving strategies. The process has received its name because it involves figuring out the "ends," or goals, that you want to attain and then devising certain "means," or strategies, for reaching them. In general, as you solve the subproblems, you continually reduce the difference between your original state and your goal state. Suppose your larger goal in playing Pac-Man is to beat the previous high score. Rather than going for this largish goal all at once, it would make much more sense to break up the problem into a number of smaller problems. These might include (1) reaching the first energizer and consuming a monster, then (2) completing a board and receiving a new maze with fresh dots, then (3) capturing the strawberry symbol. Mastering each of the subproblems gets you closer and closer to your ultimate goal. Put another way, as you complete each subproblem, you continue to reduce the difference between your original state (being a novice at Pac-Man) and your goal state (beating the previous score). You have used a means-ends analysis.

In everyday life we use means-ends analyses so often that we often take them for granted. If you must pick up a friend who is arriving tomorrow at the airport and your car has broken down, you might divide your problem into two subproblems: (1) borrowing a car and (2) getting yourself to the airport. Once the first subproblem is solved, the difference between your original state and your goal state is substantially reduced. Again, you have used a means-ends analysis.

In some instances, means-ends analysis may not be the best approach, or can even mislead you. This occurs when the solution to a problem depends on temporarily *increasing* the difference between the original state and the goal state. For example, assume that you have identified the consuming of an energizer as a first step in your ultimate plan of eventually beating the high score for the day. The consuming of an energizer is your first subgoal, and it is natural to think that you would want to move the joystick in the direction of the nearest energizer. But it sometimes makes sense to first move the joystick away from the energizer rather than toward it (for example, if there is a monster between Pac-Man and the energizer). In this instance you temporarily increase the difference between your original state and the goal state. With some games this process actually enhances your chances of winning. Discovering that a move away from the goal will actually lead you to your ultimate goal involves truly creative problem solving.

Expert Learning

What distinguishes an expert at some skill from a novice? We've seen some of the components that go into becoming an expert: you have to be a problem solver to figure out the rules of the game, you have to devise strategies to optimally accomplish a variety of goals, and you have to attach appropriate motor responses to stimuli. In addition, particularly when the skill of interest is video game playing, you must also learn to perceive game situations as complete units.

What's meant by this? Psychologists talk of perceiving and processing "chunks." A chunk is anything stored in long-term memory as a unitary whole. For instance, the letter string MGAE is perceived as four separate letters—four chunks. But the same letters presented as GAME are perceived as one word —one chunk. The fewer the chunks you have to process in order to accomplish some task, the more efficiently the task can be done.

Various studies have linked the acquisition of expertise in game playing to the fusing of many small chunks into fewer larger ones. Consider chess. In one experiment, various board positions were shown either to chess experts or to chess novices. The board positions were either random configurations of the chess pieces or they derived from actual games. Later the subjects had to reproduce the board positions they had seen. Neither the novices nor the experts could reproduce the random board configurations very well. The novices couldn't reproduce the actual game configurations very well either, but the experts could.

The boards involved perhaps twenty pieces. Apparently, however, the experts saw the game configuration boards as a small number of chunks, because any configuration resulting from an actual game was bound to be very similar to some configuration that the experts had seen many times before. This wasn't true for the novices; hence for them twenty pieces constituted about twenty separate chunks. The random board configurations were unfamiliar to everyone and were thus perceived by all as many chunks. The general principle is: The fewer the number of chunks in some stimulus, the easier is that stimulus to deal with.

The same principle can be applied to the learning of a video game. Take a complex game like Defender. The novice is overwhelmed by what takes place on the screen. Each component—each humanoid, each mutant, each stretch of terrain—constitutes a separate chunk. It takes a good deal of time to analyze all these chunks, and thus the novice is slow to respond and is quickly defeated. As you become expert, however, you begin to fuse all these chunks into fewer, bigger chunks, and begin to see not individual objects but all the objects together as situations. Since a situation is only one chunk, it's easy to analyze, and you can respond to it rapidly and easily.

Designing New Games

Most video game futurists do not seem to be taking into account the human cognitive system. Instead they emphasize what characters are likely to have the appeal of Pac-Man. In an article in *Psychology Today* writer Dan Gutman speculates on what it is about Pac-Man that made him the biggest cultural hero between John Lennon and E.T.[14] He speculated that the cute, cuddly character, who was involved in an essentially nonviolent game, was especially appealing to women, and he easily chewed up millions of their quarters. Although there may be relatively fewer women at the arcades, when they do go, they seem to enjoy Pac-Man. As for candidates for a future Pac-Man, Gutman proposed "Q*Bert," a mangy-looking, noselike creature who hops on a pyramid made of cubes, trying to make

[14]D. Gutman, "Finding an Heir for Pac-Man," *Psychology Today* 17 (March 1983): 10.

them all the same color. Every time Q*Bert hops on a new cube it changes color. Or, if not Q*Bert, then "Domino Man," who weaves his trail of dominoes through the congested shopping-center parking lot. His major role in life is to protect the trail from the Bumbling Bag Lady and the Reckless Little Boy and his hot-rod shopping cart. Or, if not Q*Bert or Domino Man, then perhaps "Millipede," who must defend its homeland from hordes of marauding insects. Perhaps the cute, cuddly characters are what draw some people to the games, but it seems likely that other considerations would be far more important.

Just as video game players may well wish to think about which cognitive abilities are required when devising a strategy, video game designers may wish to consider what cognitive strategies will be involved in any new game they might consider designing. Most probably they would consider an existing game and realize that there's some cognitive component—or set of components—that the playing of this game doesn't really require. Thus, if some modification of the game could be designed that *would* require those missing components, the game would be that much more complicated and that much more interesting. Let's look at an example of how this might work.

GROUND-LEVEL PAC-MAN

Certain of the games—Pac-Man and Defender, for example —are especially exciting and fast-moving, requiring fast reactions and fine-tuned eye-hand coordination. Others—for example, some of the "adventure," maze-running games—are slower-moving but more intellectually appealing, making much greater demands on memory (remembering where you are, where various rooms are, where you've left various objects, how to go about achieving some goal, and so on). Further, some of the adventure games stretch the imagination, allowing you to fantasize yourself into a "real-life" situation. Imagine a game in which you were *in* the Pac-Man maze, instead of looking down at it. You would be swept down the corridors gobbling up dots wherever you found them, evading the monsters, and, in general, doing what Pac-Man usually does in a Pac-Man game. From your point of view, of course, many things would have changed relative to the normal Pac-Man situation. Lacking the bird's-eye view of the maze usually enjoyed by Pac-Man players, you wouldn't know where the monsters were unless they happened to appear in the corridor; thus monsters would unexpectedly leap out from behind a corner, or would be lying in wait at the next turn. Moreover, you would forget pretty quickly where *you* were in the maze since you couldn't see yourself from the outside. As might be expected, this uncertainty would lead to problems—for instance, once you had eaten a row (or, as it appeared to you, a corridor) of dots, you wouldn't quite remember where the rest of the unconsumed dots were. You wouldn't have the traditional luxury of being able to glance around and see where the energizers were and how many were left. Finally, *you* rather than your little surrogate face would be the one in danger of being obliterated at any moment.

This hypothetical invention, "Ground-level Pac-Man," might become a reality; someone will take the concept and program it because, technically, such three-dimensionality is entirely feasible. In fact, someone has more or less thought of this idea. In Disney's box-office hit *Tron*, the central character is a man called Flynn, who is an expert computer programmer as well as a world-class video game player. During most of the movie, Flynn is trapped inside a video game trying to get out. As he zips through corridors, enemies continually try to attack him. In the end—of course—he frees himself.

CHAPTER 4

THE ARCADE SUBCULTURE

People get involved in the arcade subculture for a great variety of reasons. To illustrate some of them, we will invent a teenager named Paul. In our many conversations with people about the games and about others they know who are drawn to the games, the general qualities and life experiences we ascribe to Paul came up again and again. Later we will introduce Marlene, a similarly derived character.

Socializing in the Video Parlor

So to Paul. Let us say that he is a fifteen-year-old high school student who always had difficulty interacting with other people. When he was younger he got into fights with just about everyone. He was withdrawn and he didn't do well in school. His parents, both very busy, had little time to spend with their son—they acknowledged his existence mainly by responding to phone calls complaining that Paul had been throwing rocks at passing cars or harassing younger children. When this happened, they'd tell Paul not to do these things any more, or sometimes they'd make him stay in his room all day Saturday. There he would indulge himself in hours of playing records. He was also using drugs—beer and marijuana for the most part, but occasionally something a little more exotic, such as speed or angel dust.

One day Paul wandered into Arnold's Video Arcade, where he discovered Defender, Asteroids, and Donkey Kong. This was a brand-new world for Paul, and he took full advantage of it. He'd eagerly await his paycheck from his part-time job at the local gas station so he could convert it into quarters and head for Arnold's. He no longer cared about picking fights or throwing rocks. He stopped worrying about whether his busy parents really loved him or not. Paul's pleasures were simple: he enjoyed playing video games and would play them for hours on end. He lost interest in drugs and rock 'n roll, which was just as well since he was spending all his money at Arnold's and there wasn't anything left for these former pleasures.

Paul made friends easily at Arnold's, and for the first time in his life he felt genuinely happy. Aside from school and the gas station, Paul's whole life revolved around video games and Arnold's Video Arcade. Even when his friends weren't around, Paul still hung around the arcade, because he loved it there. He had friends—not only his human companions, but, as we'll see presently, the video games themselves.

The reasons teenagers—a main audience for the games—hang out at video parlors may not be all that different from the reasons older folks hang out at bars and coffee houses and office water coolers. It's done largely for social companionship and entertainment. But for the teenagers, there is an additional reason. An easy way for them to rebel—to distinguish themselves from their parents—is to concentrate on the pursuit of activities that are different from those of their parents. Such activities can't be too weird, or the participant would be a nonconformist—anathema to a teenager. The most reasonable activities are those on the cutting edge of culture—activities that have just entered the culture but haven't entered far enough to be acceptable to everyone, to parents in particular. So, for example, rock 'n roll music first became popular among teenagers in the 1950s and 60s—and, true to form, their parents hated it. Now these very teenagers are themselves becoming parents of teenagers. It would never do for these new teenagers to accept the old rock 'n roll that their parents like. Instead they are turning to punk rock and new wave—and video games. Anything to be different.

THE VIDEO PARLOR AS MEETING GROUND

American Graffiti, set in 1962, incorporated two phenomena that were then on the cutting edge of culture: the souped-up automobile and the fast-food, drive-in restaurant. In the film, the restaurant included such oddities as waitresses on roller skates. But, more important, the drive-ins served as a gathering place for teenagers.

The video arcade serves a similar role today. These "drive-ins of the 1980s" not only are novel but they are also a breeding ground for social interaction. They're places where social contact is made in a friendly atmosphere and where friendships are formed. They constitute the foundation of a subculture with its own norms, values, and patterns of communication. For example, it's acceptable to intently watch a person who's in the middle of a game of Defender but not to strike up a conversation with that person. Through the process of coming to learn the culture's norms and appropriate ways of communicating, and through the common ground for communication that the arcade provides, social norms are learned and friendships blossom. The fast-food joints of the 50s and 60s, although frowned on by many parents, served as the training ground for future social interaction. The video parlor is similar in this respect, but with a major difference.

The key element in the fast-food world was, and still is, social interaction. It's rare that people—especially teenagers—go to a fast-food joint by themselves. In the video world, however, people not only share interests with friends, they also interact with the games themselves in a very personal, and often solitary, way. One might ask what future roles are being prepared for the teenager by these curious person-game interactions, or conversely, what kind of adults these current teenagers are going to become. Will they be more solitary than the current adults? Will they live in a culture that is different from the one we know today?

As illustrated by the experiences of Paul, there is more to playing video games than simply the person-machine interaction. Rather, playing video games can involve an entire social experience. Game playing gets connected to friendship and often becomes a way of life. And yet the social experience of a video arcade, while not incompatible with the presence of human friends, doesn't require them either.

When people play a video game they often feel as if they are interacting with another person. One person we talked to in Houston's Space Port Arcade told us that "this game is my friend because he never ignores me." If you listen to people playing video games, you will occasionally hear them talking out loud. The things they say tell you something about the remarkable, humanlike qualities they ascribe to the game.

Two psychologists, Karl Scheibe and Margaret Erwin, have studied the conversations people have with video games while playing them.[1] In their study, forty students played video games while a tape recorder was poised nearby to catch any stray conversation. Some students played easy games while others played more difficult ones. Scheibe and Erwin meanwhile recorded the spontaneous verbalizations issued by the players.

Such spontaneous verbalization was frequent and, indeed, was recorded for thirty-nine of the forty players. While engaged in play, the players made an average of one comment every forty seconds. Men and women conversed with the game equally often, and they talked as much when they played a hard game as when they played an easy one. Scheibe and Erwin noted a widespread use of pronouns, which they found particularly interesting since pronouns imply both a humanization of the machine and a personal involvement with it. The most frequent pronoun was "it," as when a person said "It hates me." "It" occurred 244 times. Next most common was "he," as in "He's trying to get me," and then "you" as in "You dumb machine!" which occurred 57 and 51 times respectively. The pronoun "they," as in "They think they're so smart; I'll show them," occurred only 6 times. One player referred to the game as "Fred," and several people called it "that guy." Somewhat surprisingly, no one ever referred to the game as "she."

When Scheibe and Erwin examined the actual content of what people said to the games, they noticed that the remarks fell into a couple of major categories. Sometimes people made direct remarks to the computer, such as apologizing for responding too slowly. Occasionally the remark consisted of ordinary commentary, such as "It seems to know what I'm going

[1]K. E. Scheibe and M. Erwin, "The Computer as Alter," *Journal of Social Psychology* 108 (1979): 103–9.

to do next." Sometimes the remarks were simple exclamations such as "wow" or "c'mon" or expletives. In fact, profanity was quite common when the player wanted to express displeasure at getting beaten by the machine.

The nature of this one-sided conversation is illustrated by a portion of the remarks made by one player. She was playing a difficult game and lost to the computer seven times in a row. "Oh, rats, it got a point," she exclaimed. "Oh. God . . . Stupid thing! How does it do this? . . . Oh, shoot. It's killing me. Oooh. I lost by eight points. I think it's just leading me on. . . . Ha, ha, ha. I think I've got it fooled. No . . . this stupid machine. It's so dumb. . . . It's trying to con us into believing it knows what it's doing. Oh, come on . . . oops. . . . It's winning. I keep looking at the scores. I suppose that's healthy, huh? . . . It has a little mind. . . . Weird game. . . . Come on. I'm going to beat you. . . . I'm losing terribly at this one. I think my mind is beginning to wander. That could make life difficult. . . . Ah, well . . ."

What do we make of this conversation, with its heavy use of personal pronouns and its attribution to the game of human-like motives and actions? For Scheibe and Erwin, it constituted evidence that the players were reacting to the video games as if they were people. Players tended to talk more in an isolated setting than in a crowded one and to use more personal pronouns in reference to the computer when it was a more difficult game, that is, when the computer displayed more "intelligence." The comments showed that the players were emotionally involved in the experience to a very great degree. On occasion, in fact, a player would ask the arcade director if a real person weren't running the game.

Because of the ease with which people can come to cast the video games in the role of another person, it is a mistake to think of the games as neutral instruments in the socialization process. Video games, at least potentially, have the same power as television, the automobile, or any of the agents of socialization that exist in our society. Social scientist G. H. Mead prophesized this power long ago when he said: "It is possible for inanimate objects, no less than for human organisms, to form parts of the generalized other for any given human individual, in so far as he responds to such objects socially or in a social manner . . ."[2] By "generalized other" Mead was referring to the social group as a whole to which a person belongs. Obviously Mead believed that inanimate objects might belong to this "social group."

In fact, video games probably have more power than other previous instruments of socialization (for example, TV) to affect socialization, because of the highly interactive nature of the computers that underlies the games. Computers and computer games can literally replace other people in many respects. Indeed we find some striking differences between socialization in the video arcades and socialization in more traditional settings. For example, as anthropologist David Surrey notes, communication in the arcades—except with your close friends or with the machines themselves—is a social taboo.[3]

IS ALL THIS HEALTHY?

Paul, the fifteen-year-old video game addict, looked forward to going to the video arcade more than anything else in life. Although he never skipped school and was always home for dinner, he rarely did anything else. One can't help but wonder whether this was healthy. When a teenager narrows his life like this, excluding so many other activities, should we worry about

[2]G. H. Mead, *Mind, Self, and Society from the Standpoint of a Behaviorist* (Chicago, Ill.: University of Chicago Press, 1934), p. 213.
[3]D. Surrey, "It's, Like, Good Training for Life," *Natural History* 91 (November 1982): 70–83.

him? To answer this question, it's necessary to have some concept of what it means to be healthy. Because the concept of psychological health is complex, we can't define it in simple terms. Rather we must rely on several criteria to decide. Here's one reasonable set:[4]

1. Is the behavior good for the person?
2. Is the person in touch with reality?
3. Is the person's behavior markedly different from the norm?

We can talk about video game playing in the context of these three criteria.

Is the behavior good for the person? Naturally this depends on what we mean by "good." In order for Paul's game playing to be considered good, it must not get in the way of his ability to deal effectively with the world. Is Paul able to pursue his needs, to avoid unpleasant situations, to seek rewards in a way that doesn't harm others? If game playing is associated with positive feelings such as self-confidence, self-respect, and self-acceptance, then it is probably good behavior. If it is associated, on the other hand, with negative feelings such as self-hatred, isolation, and anxiety, then it is probably bad behavior. We don't mean to say that a person can never experience negative feelings associated with some good behavior; naturally this will occasionally happen. When we mourn the loss of a loved one, we experience negative feelings, but even these feelings are inappropriate if they last too long.

Given these guidelines, we'd note that Paul's video game playing is associated with positive feelings, and they don't interfere with school or the other things he must accomplish. Therefore, we might reasonably conclude that game playing is at least not bad for him.

[4]J. Freedman, *Introductory Psychology* (Reading, MA: Addison-Wesley, 1977).

But with a slightly different set of facts, we'd conclude that the games are bad. Sixteen-year-old Marlene—a composite, as you will recall—found herself playing video games about as much as Paul, but she usually skipped school to go to Arnold's Video Arcade. She often stole money from her mother's purse to finance her video habit, and once she snatched the wallet out of a jacket that another player had left on a nearby stool. After a few hours at the video parlor, she would typically go home feeling anxious and fearful. Her mind would be focused on one thing alone—how to ransack her Mother's purse again without being found out. She thought she was clever; she typically took just coins here and there, and then a few dollar bills. She never took it all, for fear of being discovered. She managed to countervene attacks of guilt by convincing herself that everyone did this, and so it was all right. When her mother finally found out what was going on, all hell broke loose in Marlene's family. Among other things, Marlene was interviewed by a psychologist, whereupon she said she was glad she was finally caught: life had been too much like walking a tightrope. In Marlene's case, her behavior had become extreme, and her attachment to video games was taking over her life. It's reasonable to think of this situation as unhealthy.

Is the person in touch with reality? The second criterion for whether game playing is healthy involves the degree to which it interferes with a person's ability to perceive the world accurately. This isn't to say that normal, healthy people always perceive the world accurately; in many instances they do not. But there are often special circumstances that can explain isolated cases of faulty perception. In cases of extreme stress— for example, after witnessing a crime or being involved in an automobile accident—our ability to function mentally may be impaired. We may momentarily see the world inaccurately.

But if a person's game playing (or anything else) consistently gets in the way of accurate perception of the world or accurate assessment of one's responsibilities, then the person will not be able to function well, and we might properly think of the person as mentally disturbed. When Marlene began to see the world as filled with people who steal from others to finance their video habits, she had, to some degree, lost touch with reality.

Is the behavior markedly different from the norm? The third criterion for whether a behavior is healthy must be viewed in terms of the norms of the society in which the person lives. There is, of course, no one "right" way to relate to video games. Some people never play them. Others play many hours a day and could perhaps be classified as video addicts. The surveys show that between these two extremes fall millions of Americans. Since many individuals can be found who play little or none at all, and many who play a great deal, we would not classify these people as deviating from the norm. Conceivably we could find an individual who spent every waking moment playing video games and we might reasonably declare that such extreme behavior was categorically unhealthy. But short of this, we will probably not be able to say that game playing violates this third criterion for mental health. If we did, we would also have to say the same about an athlete who trains five hours a day for ten years in order to reach the Olympics.

Video Games as a Mass Phenomenon

For Paul, playing video games involved an entire social experience. Looking at the social side of video games leads naturally to a conception of the games as examples of what social scientists call collective behavior. We typically speak of collective behavior as occurring when large numbers of people act to-gether with a common orientation. The participants in such behavior don't have to actually be congregated together, as they might be in a football stadium. Rather they could be physically separated as they are when they watch that same football game on television. The common focus of attention, or orientation, could be based on the desire to produce perma-nent social change, as in the nuclear freeze movement. Or it could be based on the need for sheer entertainment, as in a rock concert.

FASHIONS, FADS, AND CRAZES

Most analyses of collective behavior include some discussion of crowds—large numbers of people who are physically near one another and who have a common focus of attention. It is here that one can find analyses of panics of escape, such as occurred in Chicago's Iroquois Theater on a December after-noon of 1903 when someone yelled "fire" in a crowded thea-ter.[5] But the video phenomenon is not really a crowd phenom-enon per se. Rather it's a form of mass behavior that is more akin to a fad, a fashion, or a craze. How do they compare to other fashions, fads, and crazes that have overtaken us? Are they here to stay?

Fashions are always changing, being largely influenced by constant exposure to the mass media, degrees of affluence, and frequent contact with other people. Why are people motivated to follow the current fashions? Many answers have been sug-gested: people's wish for adventure and novelty; their desire to display symbols of success, status, and prestige; rebellion against the standards of the majority society; compensation for inferiority; and a strong need for power. Figuring out why a

[5]R. Brown, *Social Psychology* (New York: Free Press, 1965).

particular fashion is adopted while so many others are rejected is an exceedingly difficult task.

Fads, as sociologists construe them, are even more ephemeral and unpredictable. Of course, something can start as a fad and then become more permanent—like blue jeans and bingo games. But for the most part, fads pop up, spread rapidly, and then disappear. This has happened, for example, with hula hoops, Mohawk haircuts, and pet rocks.

Some social scientists have suggested that a fad must seem to be novel and must be broadly consistent with the times and particularly with modern values. Fads are generally accelerated by widespread publicity, often in the form of advertising. A decade ago, for example, the curious fad of "streaking" (running in the nude in public places) suddenly came into being. In those days streakers ran across television screens and basketball courts. Male streakers streaked through female dormitories and females streaked back. Streakers sprung up in the most unlikely places, and then almost as quickly as the fad began, it was over. Why did this fad occur? One possibility is that 1974, when the fad erupted, was a socially and politically difficult time in the United States: Richard Nixon had resigned and we were just experiencing the deep shock of the first oil crisis. The rebelliousness of streaking provided some contrast and relief.

The final type of mass behavior, the craze, refers to the involvement of a mass of people in one particular activity. Sometimes this takes the form of mass hysteria. Crazes usually involve larger sums of money than fads or fashions and are thus more serious. So the Florida land boom of the 1920s and the feverish run on the banks in the 1930s are good examples. The tulip mania of seventeenth-century Holland was probably the maddest craze of all.

94

Fashions, fads, and crazes all have to do with actions or artifacts that enjoy a rapid rise in popularity followed by an abrupt decline. Some have argued that the typical curve for these cultural phenomena resembles the curve for an epidemic disease. First there is a latent period during which the idea is present in the minds of a few people but doesn't seem to be spreading. Next there is an explosion period in which the number of people adopting the idea grows at an enormous rate. Finally there is a period in which immunity to further infection develops.

The spread of fads and other kinds of mass behavior is most common in urban areas, particularly among young people. As we've noted, adolescents in particular tend to be always on the lookout for ways to upset and shock their elders. Often the behavior embodied in a fad provides exactly the means of doing so. Although fads and crazes have occurred throughout history, two features of modern Western culture fuel them even faster: the relative affluence that permits ever more costly social experiments and the emergence of widespread communication networks—TV, radio, and telephones—that permit their rapid spread.

Where do video games fit into the picture? Will they show the typical curve—a rise in popularity, followed by an abrupt decline? Or will their fate be more like that of television or football, both of which came and stayed? To answer this question, one might analyze the kinds of cultural phenomena that have survived and the kinds that have not. One might develop a set of features that characterize the survivors from nonsurvivors. Perhaps, for example, a feature like "complexity" might apply more to the items that survived than those that didn't. For example, football and television are complex phenomena, whereas fads—hula hoops, miniskirts, and goldfish swallowing, for example—are limited in how complex they could ever become.

But another feature is perhaps the most important of all. Unlike hula hoops and miniskirts, video games are intimately linked to computer technology. We'll consider this linkage in greater detail in chapter 6. For the moment, let us note that video games have the capability of rapid change and adaptation, paralleling the concomitant changes in the computer and electronic industries. People won't have a chance to get bored with video games, therefore, so they're probably here to stay, at least for the foreseeable future. They may not remain in precisely their current form, but rather they are likely to evolve as new developments in the computer/electronics industries emerge. For example, Atari has already gone into a joint venture with a film company hoping to exploit the film company's genius for special effects in video game arcades across the nation.

ENTERTAINMENT

The most radical shift in entertainment and leisure has been propelled by the burgeoning electronics industry; indeed, electronics has provided us with a totally new form of mass culture. Before the electronic revolution of the early 1900s, people entertained themselves with plays, chamber music, conversation, books, and parlor games. But electricity brought with it novel entertainment media such as radio, television, and communications satellites. With these new devices, entertainment moved into the domain of mass phenomena, and many more people were able to participate in concerts, sports events, and comedy hours. And now, also associated with the electronic media, we have video games to supply us with a new form of entertainment. It is estimated that the number of game consoles already installed in U.S. homes in 1982 has reached 14 million, with game cartridge shipments in 1982 alone reaching an estimated 75 million.[6]

Video games, like many other forms of entertainment, seem to provide a source of stimulation. For many people they break up the boredom and provide a temporary escape from the problems of the everyday world.

Video Games as Models for Behavior

Should video games be compared to those other omnipresent visual media, movies and television? An important characteristic of TV and movies is that people model their behavior on what they see, and modeling behavior on what occurs in TV and movies has both good and bad consequences. From TV and movies, people learn socially approved behavior such as rescuing a person in distress or walking away from someone who is trying to pick a fight. But it's argued that TV and movies more often teach negative behavior that works to the detriment of society. The last few years have seen controversy and now an acceptance of the unwelcome possibility that antisocial behavior, such as violence, might be accelerated by exposure to such events on TV and film. Might the same be true for video games? Do video games "teach" us violence?

"Hey, Doug, take a look. . . ."

With these words twenty-one-year-old Mark Wentink tried to alert his friend, Doug Ilgenfritz, to an attractive woman who was walking nearby. But this seemingly innocent act init-

[6]M. F. Mansfield, "The Big Bang Marketing of Home Videogames," *Advertising Age,* 30 August 1982.

iated disaster. The woman's boyfriend was also walking near-by, and he made it clear that he didn't like what he had heard.

"You want trouble with me?" the boyfriend asked.

"No. Why? What did we do to you?" Mark replied.

"You want trouble, you got trouble," said the boyfriend as he drew a gun from his belt. Two other boys yelled something from a nearby car. And for this minor meddling, Mark and Doug ended up shot and killed.

The participants in this tragedy had just been to the Factoria Cinema in Seattle where they had seen a double feature of *The Warriors* and *Fighting Back*. Moments after walking out of the theater, the trouble began. *The Warriors* has been the subject of considerable controversy because of its alleged glorification of street-gang violence. Critics say this has led to "copycat violence" after showings in some cities. While not quite as controversial, *Fighting Back* is also decidedly violent.[7]

Was there any relation between the viewing of these violent films and the ensuing tragedy? Although we can never be sure in any individual case, a substantial body of evidence indicates that viewing excessive violence on the screen is associated with aggression and violent behavior among children and teenagers.[8] This evidence—which deals specifically with television but which is also applicable to movies—has been summarized in a recent report published by the National Institute of Mental Health (NIMH).[9] In one study involving more than seven hundred children, the total amount of TV viewing was correlated with conflict with parents and with fighting and delin-

[7]T. Guillen, "Shots, 2 Men Dead," *Seattle Times*, 25 May 1982.

[8]R. Reinhold, "U.S. Study Ties Youthful Behavior to T.V. Violence," *New York Times*, 6 May 1982.

[9]D. Pearl, ed., *Television and Behavior: 10 Years of Scientific Progress and Implications for the Eighties* (Washington, D.C.: Government Printing Office, 1982).

quency. Similarly, another study of three- and four-year-olds at a day-care center showed heavy viewing of violent programs to be correlated with unwarranted aggression during play.

Various theories have been advanced to account for the purported link between seeing violence on TV or in films and actually being violent. Some theories, for example, attribute the link to "observational learning." According to this idea, we learn violent behavior from watching television in much the same way that we learn social skills from watching our parents, brothers, sisters, and friends. Other theories posit that violent television causes a "change in attitude." Here the idea is that children who see violence on the screen become more suspicious and more prone to view the world as a place steeped in evil, ill will, and general malaise. Still other theories posit that viewing violence causes increases in physiological arousal, which then mediates future violent behavior. Finally, there is the "justification" hypothesis: watching violence on TV provides the justification, and therefore the impetus, for carrying out aggressive behavior in people who already have a violent nature.

The NIMH report clearly reflects the government's low opinion of television. Calling it a "beguiling force," the report identifies TV as a major socializing agent of American children. The potential is there to educate people, to teach them good nutritional and health habits, and to improve family relations. But sadly, say the critics, this potential has gone largely unrealized.

What analogies can we draw between TV and video games? At least one well-known psychologist, Philip Zimbardo, has worried about the social effects of video game violence, pointing out that ". . . the video games that are proving so addictive to young people may not only be socially isolating but may actually encourage violence between people."[10] Another eminent psychologist, Carl Rogers, worries that the popular video games of missiles and satellites falling on cities constitute a trivialization of the horror of nuclear war. He watched members of a family playing such a game: the skylines of cities were on the lower edge of the screen and missiles kept falling from the top of the screen. The player's goal was to stop them in midair and explode them, but often a missile slipped by, prompting a player's family member to remark, "Oops, there goes your city!" For Rogers, "We are making nuclear war thinkable by treating it as though it were just a game."[11]

For his part, psychologist Zimbardo, who seems to agree with Rogers's major premise, goes on to say that the games could be easily reprogrammed to promote cooperative play among several players—to focus on rescue operations, say, instead of destruction.

As a matter of fact, some of the games *are* beginning to focus on rescue instead of on destruction. The best known of this new genre is Donkey Kong, the video version of the film classic *King Kong*. The villain in this game is a big brown gorilla that grabs a young woman and climbs a ladder to the top of a partially completed building. The gorilla then rolls barrels down at a courageous carpenter, Mario, who is attempting to save the woman. Mario makes his way up the various levels of the building's framework by running up ramps, leaping over obstacles, climbing ladders, and jumping on moving elevators. About the only thing Mario can't do is fly. There are various prizes that Mario can win along the way—a telephone, an

[10]P. Zimbardo, "The State of the Science," *Psychology Today* 16 (May 1982): 59.

[11]C. R. Rogers, "Nuclear War: A Personal Response," *APA Monitor* 13 (August 1982): 6.

umbrella, a lunch pail, and a birthday cake. But the ultimate prize is the rescue of the maiden in distress and the reward of a free game.

Another popular "saving-people game" is Frogger. In Frogger, you are a frog. Your job is to cross a heavily traveled highway, a thin strip of land, and a densely populated river. You've got to avoid getting hit by a car, running into snakes, missing logs, and drowning in the river. You also have to watch out for crocodiles. But what really complicates your life is a very appealing Lady Frog who, once you marry, is worth a great deal to you.

Despite the popularity of Donkey Kong, Frogger, and their ilk, however, Zimbardo's worries are well founded; many of the games do focus on death and destruction. These violent games may be roughly subdivided into those involving violence toward "aliens" and those involving violence toward human beings. In the "kill aliens" category we find, for example, Defender, Galaxian, and Space Invaders.[12] In each of these games, you are pitted against an invasion of alien beings who themselves are never really seen; their presence is for the most part represented by their space vehicles. Your job is to destroy them, lest you be destroyed.

At least one of the "kill alien" games, Ripoff, has a positive side in that it encourages cooperation between two (human) players. In Ripoff, the goal is to keep alien vehicles from stealing your small, but very valuable, fuel canisters. Points are amassed for killing the aliens, and the game can be played with either one or two players. Almost all video games can in fact be played with either one or two players; however, most of these games are designed so that players take turns playing

[12]Another popular game, Asteroids, involves killing aliens only to a minor degree—most of the effort in the game is directed at the destruction of and defense against nonliving rocks of varying shapes and sizes.

solitary games. Ripoff is quite different in that the two players play simultaneously, in cooperation with each other against the aliens. The game is clearly better with two people than with one person, for two players can play more than twice as long and amass more than twice as many points as can one person playing alone. The reason for this two-person advantage is that very efficient two-person strategies can be devised; for instance, the two players can arrange their guns back to back and keep the aliens at bay almost indefinitely. We talked to Rob, one of our graduate students, who used to be an aficionado of this game until his partner moved to another city. Rob spoke quite movingly of the camaraderie he and his partner felt as they defended each other against the aliens. Perhaps such a fantasy killing can do some good if it promotes friendship and cooperation.

Despite E.T., the idea of defending ourselves against aliens may well be so deeply engrained in our collective psyche that it's futile even to worry about it. Moreover, the alien fantasy is likely to remain nothing more than fantasy—there is no reason to expect that *real* aliens will be knocking on our doors in the foreseeable future.

Much more worrisome in terms of their potentially immediate effects on our culture are the "kill people games." In Death Race, for example, you control a white car on the screen with which you relentlessly try to run over little human beings who are desperately and pathetically trying to get out of your way. In Shark Attack four divers are pursued by a shark. The player is the shark, not the divers. Soon after the bloody destruction of two major ships during the 1982 war between Britain and Argentina, a new video game materialized in Britain that involved little Argentine airplanes that tried to shoot down little British ships. The manufacturers, to their credit, did withdraw this game following an appeal to their patriotism (and their good taste), but many found it shocking that the game had appeared to begin with. These, and other games, are clearly full of violence, and violence specifically aimed at human beings. One can't help but wonder what lessons are being inadvertently, yet inevitably, learned by those who play them.

At this time, relevant research is yet to be done: we simply don't know whether excessive violence in video games is associated with aggressive and violent behavior among people. Some researchers take the optimistic view that video games are sufficiently fantasylike—detached from actual reality—that, unlike more realistic and plausible TV shows and films, they won't lead to modeling of violent behavior. Berkeley anthropologist David Surrey is one of these optimists. He quotes young arcade players on the topic: "Even though I'm shooting, it's not violent," says one Galaga player. "It's the challenge of beating the objects on the screen." Another of Surrey's interviewees is more explicit. In response to the question "Are you killing aliens?" he replies, "I just play it for the skill. It's like a sport. Like playing basketball. I could be wiping out chairs; doesn't have to be aliens. It could be television sets, as long as it moves."

Despite these sanguine observations, however, the question of whether the games promote violence is still open. And there is another broader question. What attitudes in general are these games teaching us about life on Earth? Again, the relevant research hasn't yet been done regarding video games. However, a good deal of research *has* been done with TV. Let's look at one recent study.

In studying the effects of TV on society, social scientists have moved beyond the link between violence on the tube and crime in the streets. University of Pennsylvania researcher

George Gerbner[13] has taken up a much deeper question. His interest is in how television conditions us to think—about women, about minorities, about the elderly, and about other social groups. Gerbner's study has led him to an ominous conclusion: heavy watchers of television are getting a grossly distorted picture of reality.

In his Pennsylvania study, people who watched more than four hours of TV a day (heavy viewers) were compared to those who watched less than two hours a day (light viewers). The two groups were found to have very different conceptions of the real world. For example, on prime-time television, most of the characters are male. Women are portrayed as weak and passive, deriving their influence only from their connection to powerful men. Usually they are lovers or mothers. As married mothers, they rarely work outside the home. Yet in the real world, more than 50 percent of married women with children work outside the home. Heavy TV viewers are more likely to think that most married mothers stay home all day, in accord with the image that is depicted on TV. Their attitudes about women are more stereotypical and sexist. For example, they are more likely than light viewers to believe that women belong in the home and that the running of the country should be done by men.

The elderly are a second group for which television's distorted depictions reinforce negative stereotypes. On television they appear only rarely, and when they do appear, they are cast as silly, helpless, stubborn, and sexually inactive. Heavy viewers tend to believe that these negative characteristics are generally true of older people.

Like television, video games are beguiling. They have the

[13]G. Gerbner et al., "Charting the Mainstream: Television's Contributions to Political Orientations," *Journal of Communication* 32, no. 2 (1982): 100–127; Gerbner's work is also described in H. F. Waters, "Life According to TV," *Newsweek*, 6 December 1982, pp. 136, 137, 140, 140b.

potential for being a major socializing agent of American children. But in addition to promoting violence and negative attitudes, they could, by the same token, be used to educate, promote health, and teach other values that are mostly considered to be good. The issues posed by these remarks lead us naturally to the question of what it is that people learn from the screen and how the games might be used in more constructive ways. We'll consider this issue in the next chapter.

Who Plays Video Games?

As part of his exploration of the video game world, David Surrey observed who walked into the arcades. His findings: the arcades attract a wide variety of customers. To give the flavor of this variety, he described in some detail the twenty-four-hour weekday sequence likely to be found in an arcade in New York City or Philadelphia. From midnight to dawn, the crowd is virtually all male, with players being mostly in their early twenties. From 7 to 9 A.M., the "Suits"—businessmen in their early thirties—arrive for a quick game before work. They too are mostly males. From 9 to noon, more informally dressed persons arrive—again mostly male. From noon to 2 P.M., the Suits return for a lunch break. Not until after 2 do a noticeable number of teenage females arrive—but, Surrey notes, they are often relegated to the cheerleader role.

The arcades may be attracting a wide variety of people, but most of them are males. In fact, three social scientists recently described the video arcade as a "den of teenage male culture."[14] In an informal survey conducted on busy Saturdays in

[14]S. Kiesler, L. Sproull, and J. Eccles, "Second Class Citizens?" *Psychology Today* 17 (March 1983): 43.

a suburban Pittsburgh shopping mall, the video arcades were found to be populated overwhelmingly by boys. Out of approximately 175 individuals who were counted, only 30 were girls. While a few groups of girls played together, most girls were with boys, and even then their main role was to admire the performance of their boyfriends—the cheerleader role noted by Surrey. Not once did the Pittsburgh researchers see a girl playing alone.

These observations were reinforced by a recent survey in Minneapolis.[15] After surveying 2,000 video game players in several age groups, it was concluded that heavy players (those who played at least once a week) were mostly teenage males.

What are the consequences of the den of male culture, both for the men who populate the arcades and for the women who do not? If video games have the potential for being a major socializing agent of American culture, and this potential is realized, then boys and girls may be socialized very differently. Boys may model themselves after the video characters while girls, who lack equivalent exposure, may not. However, a more troubling possible consequence revolves around the computer revolution. According to the Pittsburgh study, many children receive their initiation into the world of computers by playing video games in the arcades or at home. A majority of children who have home computers, in fact, use them to play games, along with other activities. The games, then, provide the first taste of the computer and thus serve as a first step into the computer world. Since computer literacy is becoming increasingly essential in most jobs, children who are exposed to computers early in life acquire an advantage over those who are not. The boys who outnumber girls in the arcades will be boys who outnumber girls in the adult world of computers. According to

[15]"Who Plays Video Games? You'd Be Surprised," *U.S.A. Today*, 24 March 1983.

the Pittsburgh researchers, this bias may lead to a gap in competence and confidence between boys and girls and will undoubtedly result in the girls of today becoming "second-class citizens" in our computer society. Video game companies are currently spending countless hours planning ways of gathering such neglected players as very young children, girls, and mothers into the fold.[16] Of course, the companies have their own economic reasons for this strategy. But, assuming that the companies succeed, a potentially grave social split may be averted.

Video Offshoots

Like television, video games seem to be here to stay, and they will undoubtedly spawn changes in our society and in our culture. We've already discussed some of the important ones —the potential for social isolation and for modeling behavior are examples. But culture is determined by many minor influences as well as by a few major ones, and video games have contributed to various minor facets of life as well. Here are some that have recently come to light.

One company has announced that it's now marketing a new line of "adults only" games, video analogues to pornographic movies. The characters in these games must traverse obstacle courses in order to achieve various salacious rewards. The long-term effects of these games aren't really clear, but the generally unpredictable nature of video games may engender new views of and attitudes toward sex. Public outrage toward these games seems to be more pronounced than it is toward more standard

[16]P. Nulty, "Why the Craze Won't Quit," *Fortune Magazine,* 15 November 1982, p. 114.

instruments of pornography such as "adult bookstores" and X-rated movies. In the city of Seattle, for example, there has been a long truce between its X-rated movie district and its general populace. But with the impending arrival of X-rated video games, boycotts were organized against the computer stores that had announced plans to market the games.

All this hue and cry might seem odd, considering that pornographic movies exploit and demean actual persons (the actors) whereas pornographic video games consist only of cartoon fantasies. We talked to some people involved to one degree or another in the woman's movement, and they provided us with some perspective on the issue of why the pornographic games represented such a threat. First, these women pointed out, pornographic movies are passive. Pornographic video games, in contrast, are, like all video games, active. The player is in control; playing the video games is seen as providing some kind of "practice" for engaging in the demeaning pornographic acts themselves. Second, the potential audience for video games is seen as growing at a very rapid clip, which leads to visions of the pornographic games appearing in everyone's living room within the next few years. Finally—and perhaps most important—video games are generally associated with young kids. This association produces a particularly strong reaction when pornography seems about to enter the picture.

One rather surprising spinoff of the video game craze is a new kind of pain, which has been variously termed "Space Invaders' Revenge" and "Pac-Man Elbow." Several rheumatologists have found that repeated video game button-bashing, paddle-twisting, and joystick pushing can cause skin, joint, and muscle problems. In one survey of 142 arcade players, 65 percent complained of calluses, blisters, or sore tendons. Other players have complained of numbness of the fingers, hands, and elbows. Georgia rheumatologist Gary Myerson speculates that the problems could be alleviated if players wore gloves to ease friction. However, it's unlikely that the players will actually do this. Most have simply adopted the American sports ethic: "if you don't hurt, then you really haven't worked at it." Somewhat more seriously, the October 1982 issue of *Video Games* magazine reported on the death of one video gamer. He was eighteen years old, likable, apparently healthy, and an A student. He was good at games and especially at Berzerk. He had gone to an arcade with a friend. Within fifteen minutes, he had written his initials twice in the "Top Ten." Then, bored with the game, he turned to play another one. He dropped a single quarter into the machine and collapsed, dead of a heart attack.

The intrusion of video games into health-related issues has not been restricted to physical maladies. In September 1982 the *Journal of the American Medical Association* reported a curious new psychiatric disorder that the authors termed "Space Invaders Obsession."[17] The victims of this disorder were men about to be married, and it took the form of a fourfold (or greater) increase in the playing of Space Invaders in the few weeks preceding the marriage. One man even insisted that the honeymoon be postponed for a few hours so that he could get in a few more games. The authors, researchers at the Duke University medical center, asserted that the principal goal of the game—defending a home base against aliens—took on a special symbolic significance in the face of an impending marriage. (It was also reported that, for whatever reason, game playing dropped dramatically following marriage.)

Reports of video game–related crime are beginning to appear. A recent Associated Press story, for example, tells of a thirteen-year-old boy in Des Moines, Iowa, who resorted to

[17]D. R. Ross, D. H. Finestone, G. K. Lavin, letter, *Journal of American Medical Association* 248 (Sept. 1982): 1177.

constant burglary in order to support his Pac-Man habit. The detective covering the case reported that ". . . he started about 9 in the morning, committed the burglaries, went to the bank [for quarters] and then played Pac-Man until he had to go home." In *Invasion of the Space Invaders,* British author Martin Amis notes other similar cases: in the normally low-crime country of Japan, a twelve-year-old boy held up a bank with a shotgun, demanding only coins—no bills. Cases of children becoming prostitutes specifically to earn money for video games have cropped up in several countries.

David Surrey, in his observations of video arcade behavior, notes that the arcades are the perfect location for pickpockets. Surrey quotes one source: "In my business, you go where the marks are and this is where it's at. They're into zapping these machines. . . . This may seem strange to you, but their wallets say to me, 'it's a drag in here. Take me home.' Hey, and I'm doing a favor, too. They waste their time and money here; their old lady she gets mad. So I take their wallet once and maybe they won't come in here so much."

The publishing world has also experienced the video game phenomenon. Scores of books have appeared on video games and how to beat them; daily newspapers have started to run syndicated video game columns; and several video game magazines have been created. The magazines not only provide tips on how to play, and stories of celebration, but they also crusade against those who try to restrict video games. The question of video regulation has cropped up all over the world. Just recently, video game parlors were banned in Singapore because they allegedly cause harm to children. "We are aware of the undesirable influence these centers have on our young people," said the city's cultural minister. "Many have become addicted and waste considerable time and money on these video games."

Will the games enter high culture? The DeCordova Museum near Boston recently held an exhibit entitled "From Pong to Pac-Man," accompanying the work of Harold Cohen, a British abstract painter who has recently turned to computer-generated art. The exhibit was in two parts. The first included a selection of video games that, according to the brochure,[18]

will be interpreted as "folk art" with their own unique, vernacular language. The evolution from simple task-oriented games, to games with a proscribed story line in which the player becomes protagonist, will be demonstrated with a selection of machines dating from 1972 to the present. In evidence will be the ever increasing elaboration and realism of imagery which has developed in this ubiquitous form of "participatory television."

The second part of the exhibit included works of other contemporary artists

whose imagery is similar to that which is usually associated with video games. The screen-scape, characterized by a blank background and miniature figures acting out a mute, but violent drama are epitomized by the paintings of Nicholas Africano. The pattern-scape, reminiscent of video games like Pac-Man, in which figures are placed in a landscape of strong geometric regularity, is demonstrated by the work of Roger Brown. William Conlon's paintings exemplify the line-scape or "physics of vision," in which environments are created from perspectival lines. "From Pong to Pac-Man" will explore related visual identities in an attempt to show how the commercial vernacular languages of our society influence the fine arts.

[18]Quoted by permission of the DeCordova Museum.

CHAPTER 5

LEARNING FROM THE SCREEN

In the last chapter, we considered television as a model for investigating the influences that video games might have on our culture. We'll use the same strategy here, focusing on learning and education. First we'll look at the allegedly adverse effects that TV may have on learning and the potential educational advantages of TV. Then we'll discuss computer games and education, arguing that the educational potentialities of the games are enormous. Even now it's easy to identify a number of indirect educational benefits the games provide.

TV as Teacher

Numerous surveys indicate that the average child watches about five hours of television a day. Between the ages of two and five, very impressionable years, many children spend almost two-thirds of their waking life watching TV. Older children often spend more time watching TV than they do attending school. Are children learning anything useful during all these hours? Some critics suggest that the answer is no, that little formal learning takes place while we watch since TV doesn't really engage our minds. Learning is done most efficiently when we are forced to use the material being presented —when we have to repeat it, study it, write it down, paraphrase it, and digest it. The fact that most of us can't remember anything from a TV show that we saw a year or two ago—or even more recently—suggests how little we actually retain from TV.

Does this kind of evidence *prove* that we don't learn from watching TV? No, and in fact quite a different view comes from Gavriel Salomon, an educational psychologist at the Hebrew University of Jerusalem, who claims that what children learn from TV depends on the show.[1] Citing the work of Yale psychologist Jerome L. Singer,[2] Salomon points out that children attend more to the fast pace of *Sesame Street* but learn more, or at least remember more, from *Mr. Rogers' Neighborhood*. Apparently the fast pace and changing of scenes in *Sesame Street* do not allow sufficient time for processing and memorizing the information, even though the children attend to it. In other words, the children may like the show better, but they do not learn more from it.

This doesn't imply that children learn nothing from *Sesame Street*. Salomon had the unique opportunity to study children who were first being exposed to the program when it was

[1]G. Salomon, *Interaction of Media, Cognition and Learning* (San Francisco: Jossey-Bass, 1981).

[2]J. L. Singer, "A Preschooler's Comprehension and Play Behavior Following Viewing of *Mr. Rogers* and *Sesame Street*," Paper presented at the American Psychological Association, San Francisco, 1977.

brought to Israeli television in the fall of 1971. He was especially curious about whether exposure to the program enhanced the development of any specific skills.

Since the program was being broadcast nationally and was very popular, it was almost impossible to have a control group —a group of children who didn't view it at all. Instead the children in Salomon's study were allowed to watch the program as much as they wanted and were tested at several different times. In this way, children who watched the show a great deal could be compared to those who watched it very little.

The program was broadcast in English with a Hebrew voice-over, but despite this drawback, it had wide appeal. Over 90 percent of the children claimed to watch at least parts of *Sesame Street,* and about half claimed to watch the entire program all the time. Did the heavy viewers perform differently from the light viewers on tests of mental ability? The answer appears to be yes. The children who watched the show more tended to perform better on subsequent tests of mental skills such as letter matching, number matching, and picture/-number matching than did their little colleagues who watched it less. In these tests a child selects the correct letter or number that matches a given letter, number, or picture. *Sesame Street,* of course, emphasizes just these sorts of skills.

In a later study, children were randomly assigned to watch either eight hours of *Sesame Street* on a wide screen or to watch an equal number of hours of adventure and nature films. They watched these films one hour a day for eight days and were then tested. In this experiment, the *Sesame Street* group performed significantly better than the adventure-film group on a number of mental tests. Thus we can conclude that the children do learn something (as opposed to nothing) from watching *Sesame Street.* At the very least they learn the specific skills that the program has been designed to teach, and they do so not only under controlled experimental conditions but also under normal viewing circumstances.

Do children learn any skills beyond those that are specifically taught by the TV program? Even if the answer to that question turns out to be yes, there will remain an inherent problem with learning from TV. This problem—the passive nature of the medium—is interesting in the context of this book, because it is a problem that is *not* inherent in computer-based learning systems such as video games.

One of the authors (GL) had some firsthand experience with the results of TV-bred students. One year, while teaching his statistics class at the University of Washington, GL noticed that the students seemed to be more passive than they had been in previous years. They didn't ask questions; they didn't respond as well to his jokes; in general, they just sat there listening to what he had to say, occasionally taking notes. At first, GL was baffled by this seemingly inexplicable change in his students' behavior. One day, though, it dawned on him that this class was the first he had taught that had grown up watching *Sesame Street*. GL reasoned that this experience—hundreds of "TV as teacher" hours—may have substantially altered his students' expectations about what the relationship between teacher and pupil was supposed to be.

With a passive teaching device, you can't determine if or how well the child is responding. It isn't possible to provide individual feedback. And you can't easily tailor your teaching to the learner's prior knowledge because you don't have any idea how much prior knowledge the child has. Gavriel Salomon, among others, discovered that the levels of knowledge and skill that children bring with them to the viewing situation will affect if and how they benefit from television. But the television does not have this information about an individual viewer and thus, obviously, can't be responsive to it.

Many different types of experiments confirm the importance of active involvement in the learning process. One classic study was done at MIT.[3] In this study, two kittens from the same litter were placed in identical surroundings. One of them, the active kitten, could move around normally. Meanwhile, the active kitten's brother, the passive kitten, was restrained in a gondola chair but was moved around in such a manner that its visual experiences were identical to those of the active kitten. When not being tested, both kittens spent their time in total darkness. After only ten days, the active kitten displayed normal visual behavior, while its passive sibling behaved as if it were blind. Eventually, after several days of normal experience, the passive kitten learned normal visually guided behavior. This experiment suggests that learning, in this case perceptual learning, depends a great deal on whether the animal has an opportunity to interact with its physical environment.

Computers as Interactive Devices

The idea that active involvement spurs learning goes back at least as far as the time of Socrates. Indeed, to interact with students is the reason teachers exist in the first place. However, there are many more learners around needing instruction than there are teachers to offer it.

Twenty or so years ago, educators began to realize that the computer, with its powerful interactive abilities, might be used to aid in instruction. Thus, the concept of computer-assisted instruction (or "CAI") was born.

[3]R. Held and A. Hein, "Movement Produced Simultaneously in the Development of Visually Guided Behavior," *Journal of Comparative and Physiological Psychology* 130 (1969): 133–41.

By the mid-1960s several CAI projects were underway. One of the most ambitious was the Stanford project, under the direction of Professors Patrick Suppes and Richard Atkinson.[4] Thousands of elementary school students were involved, and a variety of scholastic subjects were taught. One, for example, was a drill-and-practice program in which the student would sit down at a teletype and type in a number and his or her first name. This information was transmitted via telephone lines directly to the computer at Stanford. The computer responded by typing the student's last name and giving him or her an arithmetic drill for the day. When the lesson was completed, the computer typed the score, the elapsed time, and said goodbye, using the student's first name ("Goodbye, Carol"). Students averaged from four to ten minutes per day at the teletype.

During the 1967–68 school year, almost 4,000 students at various elementary and junior high schools completed nearly 300,000 arithmetic lessons, covering such concepts as addition, fractions, and inequalities. Students in the program showed significant gains in the achievement of computational skills when compared to other groups of children who received traditional, noncomputerized methods of teaching. College students as well as elementary ones benefited from learning via CAI. In September 1967, thirty Stanford University students enrolled in a course of computer-assisted Russian, wherein they received instruction at computer-based terminals for fifty minutes a day, five days a week, throughout the entire academic year. Another group of students received regular classroom instruction. At the end of the first year, the computer students performed at a higher level. In addition, the motivational be-

[4]P. Suppes, "The Uses of Computers in Education," *Scientific American* 215 (1966): 207–20; R. C. Atkinson and H. A. Wilson, "Computer-assisted Instruction," *Science* 162 (1968): 73–77.

nefits of CAI were demonstrated by the finding that, compared to those receiving regular instruction, fewer of computer-taught students dropped the course.

The CAI programs of the 1960s incorporated a variety of features that, from the standpoint of educational theory, were sophisticated and beneficial. The programs kept an updated summary of each student's work. As the student worked his or her way through the curriculum material, performance was continually evaluated. The nature of the next drill was determined by how well the student did on the previous one. If the drill was too difficult, the computer automatically branched the student to easier problems. On the other hand, if the student performed well, he or she was given more difficult problems. This meant that the computer always assigned problems that were at the right level to challenge the students. Instruction was thus highly individualized in a way that classroom instruction, with one teacher and thirty, or fifty, or one hundred, or five hundred students, can never be.

Despite these advantages, the CAI project lacked some useful educational ingredients. One important one had to do with motivation. Interacting with the computer was challenging, but it was never really considered to be great fun: drill and practice was still drill and practice, even when it was administered by a shiny computer instead of by a stern human. Second, whereas the computer-aided teaching programs of twenty years ago engaged students reasonably well at the verbal level, they hardly engaged them at all at the visual level. Interaction with the computer was done completely via a teletype; there weren't the multicolored graphics and interesting sound effects that are routine facets of today's technology. Third, computers were big and expensive; indeed the CAI program for an entire school system would be run from one large, central computer. This meant that when the computer crashed or had to be turned off for maintenance, the CAI system for the entire community came to a standstill. Also, there were resource problems. If the school system had a lot of resources, both financial and technical, that could be allocated for such an exotic enterprise, things were fine; otherwise, acquisition of a CAI system simply wasn't possible. Thus an affluent, upper middle-class community such as Palo Alto, with a great deal of money to spend on education and brigades of Stanford scholars right next door interested in and working on CAI, found itself with computer instruction in abundance. But isolated, poor communities were out of luck.

Today, with the proliferation of cheap microcomputers, computer-based instructional programs have become much more available. Rather than being confined to large experimental projects, educational programs are being written and distributed by a large range of enterprises ranging from giant companies to small, basement entrepreneurs. Graphics are a central and universal feature of all computer systems, both large and small. And the distinction between games and educational programs has become much more blurred. This blurring is evident, for example, in Thomas Malone's work, which, as we saw in chapter 2, was primarily concerned with how to make the educational experience enjoyable and intrinsically motivating for the learner.

We shall return to Malone's work and discuss it specifically in the context of education in a later section of this chapter. For the moment, let us examine the work of an MIT researcher, Seymour Papert, who is currently one of the leading advocates of the computer as a tool for learning.

In a remarkable book called *Mindstorms*, [5] Papert explicitly compares learning via television and learning via the computer. With television, the child is in the position of listening to

[5] S. Papert, *Mindstorms* (New York: Basic Books, 1980).

explanations. The explanations may sometimes be perfectly engaging, but they rarely, if ever, require a response from the listener. Computers, in contrast, require a more active and self-directed learning process. Papert stresses the advantages of teaching children how to program a computer (a theme to which we shall return later), and here he has anecdotal cases of success. For example, one fifth-grade boy, Bill, had always hated math and particularly multiplication tables. "You learn stuff like that by making your mind a blank and saying it over and over until you know it" was the way he described the learning process. Although Bill spent considerable time trying to learn the tables, his performance was poor, as was his attitude. In fact, he never really mastered the tables because he never really was able to relate them to any other aspect of his life. Several of his teachers said Bill had "a poor memory," and some even speculated that he might have brain damage. But they couldn't quite reconcile this with his extensive knowledge of popular folk songs, which he could remember with no difficulty at all. Although it might be tempting to speculate that Bill's poor memory was specific to numbers, this was ruled out by his ability to easily recount reference numbers, prices, and dates for thousands of records. Given the right context, his ability to work with and remember numbers was obviously intact.

Bill started learning both simple and complex mathematics via computer, and his situation improved dramatically. With the computer, he found subjects as complex as geometry rather simple to master. He learned geometry not through the usual means but through "Turtle Geometry." In this innovative system, an object called a Turtle is the focus of the learner's attention. The Turtle is like a person in many ways. It is in a particular position and can face different directions. It's something with which the child can identify. The student can learn to talk to the Turtle via computer commands, asking it to move forward or backward, right or left. The Turtle can be made to trace a square, a triangle, a rectangle, or a circle. Bill learned to use his own body to help decide how to move the Turtle. For example, when he wanted to make a circle, he would say to himself, "When you walk in a circle you take a step forward and you turn a little. And you keep doing it." From this description, he was about to develop the necessary means to instruct the Turtle to move in a circle. Soon Bill was creating squares of different sizes, triangles embedded within circles, and complex architectural structures. By connection with movement and the navigational knowledge needed in his everyday life, Bill related to Turtle Geometry, as he did to his songs, far more than to multiplication tables. The mathematical knowledge that Bill had previously rejected finally found its way into his intellectual world.

For the most part, Papert's demonstrations of the effectiveness of computer approaches to learning have been anecdotal. Furthermore, his research involves special kinds of computer games—those expressly designed for instructional purposes. It still remains to be shown that interacting with more ordinary computer games can teach people important things.

Video Games as Learning Devices

It would be comforting to know that the seemingly endless hours young people spend playing Defender and Pac-Man were really teaching them something useful. What, for example, about "eye-hand coordination," which is becoming such a buzzword in video game magazines? Is the massive amount of practice in motor coordination going to be useful for anything besides being a better video game player? As relevant research has not yet been performed, we can only speculate about direct educational benefits. But it seems safe to say that the games provide a number of interesting and important *indirect* benefits. We'll consider four such indirect benefits before turning to speculations about direct ones.

AN INTRODUCTION TO COMPUTERS

Virtually no one denies that a thorough and sophisticated knowledge of computers is going to be necessary for getting along in society from now on. This dictum applies *a fortiori* to young children, who are going to be dealing with computers all their lives.

Increasingly, courses on computers are being taught in school, particularly from the junior high level up. Suppose a school child is presented with a new object that he or she is supposed to learn about. What provides the motivation for such learning? One very strong motivating force accrues if the object already plays a prominent role in the child's life.[6] Thus, we argue, children who play video games know that these games are computer-based, even if they have never seen an actual computer and only have a vague notion of what a computer is. However, when, sooner or later, they *are* presented an actual computer and are told that they have to learn about it, they don't do their learning in a vacuum. They know at least one thing about computers that is very important in their lives, namely, that with computers you can make video games. Thus, there is at least one thing about computers that interests the youngsters, and that provides the motivation to learn enough

[6]An example of the converse of this rule is seen in foreign language learning. American children typically have virtually no experience with speaking foreign languages. French, for example, is usually entirely unrelated to the rest of the children's lives, and they have rather little motivation to learn it. Partly for this reason, foreign language learning has become deemphasized in the U.S. over the years.

about how to program the computer to be able to create video games. It turns out, of course, that in the process of learning about how to program video games, they learn quite a bit about how the computer works in general and about how to write computer programs. This additional knowledge then provides the ability to write more general programs. Learning about computers is, in other words, a bootstrapping operation that involves an alternation of first finding out some interesting thing the computer can do and then acquiring the knowledge necessary to make the computer do it. This knowledge then provides the vision for more complex goals that require and motivate yet more knowledge, and expertise spirals upward. In any bootstrapping operation, however, there is always the problem of how to get it started in the first place. Often in educational settings, threats and cajoling are needed. In the case of computers, video games provide this start in a painless, indeed enjoyable, way.

We recently attended a party in a middle-class suburb of Seattle. At some point during the party, a group of grownups were in the basement playroom drinking and talking while, in the same room, a group of children were playing video games on a home computer. The adult discussion turned to the book we were writing, and the inevitable question was raised: Did the games that we were watching on the other side of the room teach anything useful? As it happened, we had spent that morning discussing the video-game-as-computer-introduction argument that we've just described. We presented the argument to our listeners, but it was received with a great deal of skepticism. In the middle of the discussion, twelve-year-old Scott, one of the video game players, came wandering over, software catalog in hand. We asked him why he liked video games and eventually inquired what he would choose if he could have anything in the catalog. Much to everyone's surprise, he pointed not to a specific game but to the programming module. We asked him if he knew how to program, and he replied that he didn't. "What *is* programming?" we asked, and he told us he wasn't really sure. Did they have any computers in his school? No, but he'd study computers next year in junior high. Well, if computers weren't a social focus in his school, if he didn't know how to program computers and really didn't know what programming was in the first place, why was the programming module what he most wanted? Scott replied that he did know that computer programs made video games work, and if he had the programming module, then he could learn how to program his own games. This reply provided such a perfect confirmation of our argument that the astonished adult onlookers refused to believe that we hadn't set Scott up.

Will Scott go on to become an expert programmer? Of course, we have no way of telling. However, an example of a former video game fanatic who did is provided by another composite of several players whom we interviewed. Mark, as we shall call him, had spent three years and thousands of quarters playing video games in Los Angeles's Westport Arcade. After his first year of playing, Mark became curious about how the games worked and started reading everything he could find on the topic. It became clear to him that what took place on the screen when he played the games didn't happen by magic, but rather as a result of very sophisticated computer programming. His twenty-first birthday was coming up, and he begged his parents to buy him a computer so that he could try to create his own games. After working out a complex financial arrangement with his mother, he depleted his savings account to pay for half of an Apple II. Mark immediately learned to program his new toy by reading several books and soon had made himself a simple video game. In the process he had not only learned what a program is and how to write one, but he learned a great deal about how computer graphics are generated and how information is represented inside the computer.

One unexpected surprise for Mark's parents was his desire to go back to school. He enrolled at a local junior college, majoring in computer science. To finance his education, Mark conducted a small window-washing business on the side, for which the computer came in handy. He wrote programs to keep track of his customers, the dates on which he had washed their windows, and whether their accounts were up to date. He wrote a program that sent out notices to his customers reminding them that it was time to have their windows washed again. His business flourished, even in a slow economy.

The experiences of Scott and Mark are being repeated throughout the country. Everywhere we turn, we seem to hear anecdotes of nervous, computer-shy parents being wheedled and cajoled by their children to buy computers. The children's motivation is not *always* to be able to program video games, but it seems to be in a sizable number of cases.

Of course, a series of anecdotes doesn't prove that video game playing leads to computer expertise. Perhaps only a few video game players will go on to be computer programmers. Or maybe the appropriate research will show us that many expert programmers never had anything but disdain for computer games. However, at the very least, video games are providing many people with a substantial introductory dose of computer technology.

EDUCATION-ORIENTED VIDEO GAMES

Educators have been trying to harness the astonishing motivational power of video games by designing educational computer games that resemble their arcade counterparts. Two pioneers in this area are Thomas Malone at the Xerox Palo Alto Research Center and John Frederiksen at the research firm of

Bolt, Beranek and Newman in Cambridge, Massachusetts. Malone's work is primarily aimed at generating a theory of instruction based on the intrinsically motivating elements of video games, whereas Frederiksen has actually designed some games—in particular, some that will help people who have reading problems.

Malone, whose work was discussed in some detail in chapter 2, believes that, unlike the usual learning environment, computer games create "intrinsic motivation." Such intrinsic, or self-generated, motivation is due in part to the presence of goals, of challenge, and of fantasy.

A major ingredient of video games that makes them not only fun but also ideal for learning is the well-defined goal structure that they incorporate. Imagine, for example, a child who has to learn the locations of several major cities around the world. Typical schoolroom tests have, in the past, involved indicating the major cities on a specially provided map. Some students can perform well on the test because they can visualize the world and "see" where the cities belong—that is, by using a spatial strategy. Others have succeeded by memorizing the latitudes and longitudes of the cities in question and placing the cities accordingly—a more verbal strategy. But in neither case did students generally consider this task to be "fun." Like the old arithmetic drill and practice, the geography test was labeled work.

But now imagine a computer game in which children read about a child hero who is given information about latitudes and longitudes and must use this information to solve the problem of rescuing other children from evil aliens who are holding hostages at various points around the globe. The player roams around the computer world seeking these hostages and is rewarded for each one found. Instead of being tedious, unconnected facts, existing only to be memorized in school, city locations constitute vital information, and the ability to locate the cities becomes a necessary skill for achieving the interesting goal of rescuing hostages. Moreover, the goal is part of an intrinsic fantasy, involving a child hero with whom the child-learners can strongly identify.

As we noted in chapter 2, another ingredient of the intrinsically motivating instructional game is challenge, or uncertainty of outcome. With computer games, one way to achieve this challenge is to create games whose difficulty levels shift in accordance with how well the player is doing. Difficulty will depend on such factors as the amount of time needed to reach the goal, the memory capacity required, and the response speed that is necessary. With a computer's flexibility providing the foundation, these instructional games can vary in difficulty level so that they remain forever challenging.

Stanford psychologist Mark Lepper has pointed out, however, that simply inserting "challenge" into educational material is not without its pitfalls.[7] Lepper remarks that the strategy of providing challenge can backfire if the children aren't aware of the structure of the learning material. Lepper writes, "Rather than enhancing motivation, such programs may often undermine it by leading children to perceive themselves as incapable of succeeding. As one child engaged in one of these programs commented, 'Every time I think I've got it, I just miss more of them.' " Educational material that is structured as a video game does much to remedy this difficulty. Instead of abstract problems that mysteriously increase in difficulty, some more-or-less true-to-life situation—such as being required to cut up a pizza into equal-size slices—is presented. It then

[7]M. Lepper, "Microcomputers in Education: Motivational and Social Issues," Address to the American Psychological Association, Washington, D.C., 1982.

becomes quite clear from the situation that it's harder to divide the pizza among seven people than among two people or eight people.

Given that goals and challenges are appropriately provided, why are they so captivating to people? Malone thinks it's because they engage a person's self-esteem. Success in the world of learning, like success in any other sphere of life, can make people feel better about themselves. The other side of the coin, of course, as Lepper points out, is that failure lowers self-esteem and, in so doing, can destroy a person's interest in learning. The optimal instructional game is one that has a challenging difficulty level but also minimizes the possibility of damage to self-esteem. The challenge of a game must remain inviting rather than discouraging. Computer games have the powerful potential for providing this balance on an individual basis in a way that the single teacher in a classroom full of students would find practically impossible to do.

The final aspect of the computer game that makes it especially suited for drawing people into learning is fantasy. Children love fantasy and make no bones about it. Probably most adults love fantasy, too, but they're often somewhat embarrassed to admit it. As a fantasy extreme, Malone points to Disneyland. People love Disneyland, with all its surrealistic characters and fantastic adventures. It would be natural to try to identify ways of making the learning process more like going to Disneyland. It is a challenge for educators to try to figure out how to incorporate the fantasy elements so intimately linked with the Disneyland-like experience into the world of learning.

In computer games, fantasies abound. They are created by all the "bells and whistles" of the game—the plot, the graphics, and the sound effects. Fantasies are instructionally useful for a number of reasons. For one thing, they help a learner apply old knowledge to understanding new things. For example, when playing the game Darts, which teaches about fractions, players can see right on the display screen that some objects —arrows and balloons—are placed higher or lower than others. If the connection is made between number size and position on the number line, then learners will be able to use their old knowledge about position to make inferences about the relative sizes of unfamiliar fractions.

A second advantage of fantasies is that they provide or provoke vivid images related to the material to be learned. This provides an ideal situation, since numerous psychological experiments have demonstrated that using imagery is one of the best ways to learn new material.[8] Finally, fantasies serve several emotional functions, one of which is wish fulfillment. This aspect of fantasies presents some unique problems for designers of instructional games. It isn't an easy task to predict what kinds of fantasies will be appealing to different people. Should a single fantasy be selected that is likely to appeal to the entire population? Should several fantasies be offered from which students could select their favorite? Should some types of fantasies be avoided if they could lead to special problems, for example, fantasies that provoke feelings of aggression? In theory, fantasies can be powerful ways of harnessing preexisting emotional motivations and can be used to increase interest in learning. Given these fantasies, it's easier for parents to buy games for their children that both held the children's interest and also taught them something.

Whereas Malone's work is general—it is primarily concerned with an overall theory of instruction and motivation— the work of John Frederiksen and his colleagues has been aimed at a very specific educational problem, that of improving

[8]See, for example, A. Paivio, *Imagery and Verbal Processes* (New York: Holt, 1971).

reading skills.[9] Frederiksen's past work, both theoretical and empirical, has been aimed at revealing some of the specific subskills that are involved in reading. Poor readers can be identified in terms of deficiencies in one or more of the sub-skills. Practice on the deficient subskills can then be prescribed.

As an example, some people are poor readers because they are slower (although not necessarily less accurate) than good readers at identifying specific letter groups such as *cl, ple, th,* and *gen* when these groups appear within words. Put another way, the good readers seem to be able to identify the letter groups more "automatically" than the poor readers. By "automatic" we refer to the ability to carry out some skill quickly and without paying conscious attention to it. An experienced driver can, for example, drive and hum a tune at the same time. Both of these skills—driving and humming—are automatic, and the operation of one does not interfere with the operation of the other.

Suppose that we wanted a reader, deficient in this letter-group recognition skill, to be able to practice it. To allow such practice to proceed in an enjoyable way, Frederiksen and his colleagues have devised a game called "Speed" that requires players to detect whether a target letter cluster is present within words that are presented in rapid succession. Is the cluster *th* present within *hearth?* Yes. Within *church?* No. It seems easy to do when you have plenty of time, but in the video game that the researchers developed, the players had to answer faster and faster without making too many errors.

Figure 5.1 shows the video screen as it appears at the start of a session. Notice that the letter cluster to be identified is *ler.* When the player is ready, words will be presented on the screen, one after the other, and the player's job is to hit one

[9]J. Frederiksen, B. Warren, H. Gillote, and P. Weaver, "The Name of the Game Is Literacy," *Classroom Computer News,* May/June 1982, pp. 23–27.

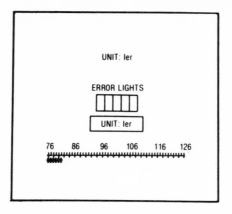

FIGURE 5.1

The video screen at the start of a session.

Reproduced from J. Frederiksen et al., "The Name of the Game Is Literacy," *Classroom Computer News* 2, no. 5 (May/June 1982): 26. Used by permission of J. Frederiksen and Pitman-Learning Inc.

button indicating yes (*ler* is present) or another button indicating no (*ler* is not present) as quickly as possible after each word appears. A "speedometer" at the bottom of the screen indicates that, initially, the words are to be presented relatively slowly—about 80 words a minute, or just slightly more than one a second. But the player will be required to speed up, reaching a goal of 126 words a minute. Each time a correct response is made, the rate at which words are shown is increased, and the speedometer needle moves to indicate this increase. Figure 5.2 shows that the player is performing well, and words are now coming at a rate of 95 per minute. As the player gets faster and faster, he or she is rewarded with a smooth increase in speed, moving in the direction of the final goal.

Suppose the player makes an error. If so, an error light comes

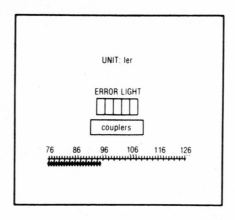

FIGURE 5.2

The student has done well, and the speedometer is up to 95 words per minute.

Reproduced from J. Frederiksen et al., "The Name of the Game Is Literacy," *Classroom Computer News* 2, no. 5 (May/June 1982): 26. Used by permission of J. Frederiksen and Pitman-Learning Inc.

on and the word presentation rate is decreased. However, whenever some number of successive correct responses is made, one of the errors is erased. If the player reaches five errors, the game ends, the player languishes in defeat, and the process begins anew. The number of errors is indicated by the number of error lights, so the player is constantly aware of how close he or she is to disaster.

All the elements of intrinsic motivation enumerated by Malone are present in this game (as well as in the other games for other subskills that Frederiksen and his colleagues have devised). In Speed, there is a clear goal, that of attaining the required speed. Feedback is constantly provided by the speedometer and error lights. The difficulty level is constantly adjusted to keep challenge at a reasonable level. There is the fantasy of driving a car, thinking perhaps of the speedometer as representing miles per hour rather than words per minute. Although research on the benefits of these games is just now underway, preliminary reports are highy encouraging. Over the course of training, many players begin with goal speeds of 110 to 120 words per minute and reach speeds of over 150 words per minute by the third or fourth time they practice a particular cluster. After training, many players have shown a dramatic improvement in other skills related to reading ability.

LEARNING PHYSICAL LAWS

To some people, the laws of physics seem intuitively reasonable, but to others they don't seem very obvious at all. Take the following hypothetical example: suppose a train were coming toward you at 60 miles per hour, and someone standing on top of the train threw a ball forward at 20 miles per hour relative to the train. How fast would the ball be going relative to you? If you answered 80 miles an hour, you would probably be among the intuitive group; if you answered 20 miles an hour, your intuitive grasp of physics might be faulty. People in the latter category, even when they learn to provide the correct answer, often seem unsure of themselves, as if the problem were beyond their real understanding.

Taking another example, look at figure 5.3 and try to answer this question: Suppose a bomber is flying north at 600 miles an hour and drops a bomb at exactly the moment it is over point X. Where will the bomb land? Again, the less intuitive person is likely to reply that the bomb would land on point X, when in fact the bomb would land to the north of the point. If you answered this question incorrectly, you are not alone. Many highly intelligent, highly educated people have the same difficulty, which actually has been awarded its own label: "naive physics."

Naive physics is a topic of a good deal of research (much of

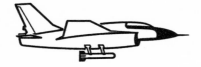

FIGURE 5.3

The naive physicist's problem: If the bomb is dropped when the plane is directly over point X, where will the bomb land?

it sponsored by the U.S. Department of Defense, which wants the recruits who operate its artillery and its nuclear generators to have a *good* understanding of physics, not a naive one). Psychologist Lepper points out that video games could potentially be used to provide an intuitive understanding of many principles of physics. He calls such games "educational simulations" in reference to the fact that physical events can be simulated on the screen by inserting the appropriate physical laws into the computer program. He refers to an example developed in a physics-learning program at the University of California, Irvine, in which lunar and solar eclipses are simulated on the computer. "In this program," Lepper notes, "students studying the mechanics of eclipses can 'experiment' with a wide variety of relative positions of the sun, earth, and moon, receiving responsive feedback after each choice." Lepper goes on to speculate about how other laws can be studied in such a way that the consequences of the laws are quite obvious. Violations of the laws could similarly be examined. Suppose a gravity simulation were changed so that gravity were governed by a simple inverse-distance relationship, rather than by an inverse-square relationship. What would happen? How would the universe be different?

While playing Sabotage one day, one of the authors (GL) was struck with his own vision of how video games could be used as physics instructors. GL noticed how perfectly realistic the little helicopters looked when they exploded and fell out of the sky. He marveled at how elegantly this perfection could be programmed, since the laws of physics could be written as equations and the equations simply inserted into the game program. GL went on to fantasize about how he would use a video game to provide a child with an intuitive understanding of physics. We will describe this fantasy in some detail, because it's an instructive and very plausible exercise in how intuitive learning of physical laws might occur.

Imagine a child (call him David) faced with the problem in figure 5.3. David, like most people naive about physics, declares that the bomb will fall on point X. David (who is assumed to have some programming capability) is then assigned the task of programming the problem on his home computer, in order to see what the falling bomb would look like. He soon completes this relatively simple job. He runs the program—and what is depicted in figure 5.4 takes place on the computer's screen. The bomb moves horizontally during the time it is still attached to the bomber. Then, when released, the bomb executes an abrupt right-angle turn and drops straight down to point X. The instant David sees this happen on the screen, he knows that something is amiss. Things just don't look like that when they fall from a moving object. Obvious failure. Back to the drawing board.

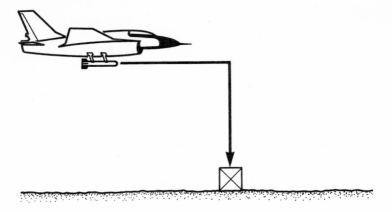

FIGURE 5.4

The naive physicist programs his solution.

It doesn't take David long to figure out a major component of his problem. In a flash of insight, it dawns on him that the bomb was originally in motion along with the bomber and, just because the two had separated, there is no reason for the bomb to abruptly cease this forward motion—although David has implicitly assumed, both in the original answer to the question and in the program he had written, that that's indeed what would happen. He quickly revises his program so that the bomb's forward motion continues after it parts company with the bomber. When David reruns the program, the bomb's descent is as depicted in figure 5.5: it is a straight line going obliquely down from the point of release. This looks much better than the original version, but it still isn't quite right.

Determined to make it look perfect, David spends several hours working on variations of the program. First he tries varying the ratio of the bomb's forward to downward speed.

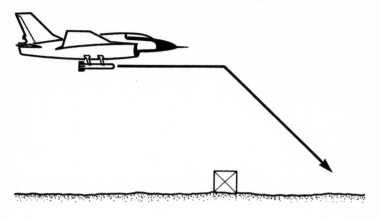

FIGURE 5.5

The naive physicist improves his solution.

This doesn't provide any direct help. The bomb's descent still takes the form of straight lines; they just go at different angles, as shown in figure 5.6. It doesn't take long (especially after dropping a few pennies from his moving hand) for David to pick up the general principle that straight lines are wrong. The bomb should curve downward; that is, its angle of descent should become progressively steeper. Looking at the various angles, it's quite evident that the steeper lines result from faster downward speeds. Thus David figured out that if the downward speed were to increase during the bomb's descent, then the bomb's path would progressively steepen and would look more the way that he knows it ought to.

How exactly to make the speed increase? The simplest thing David can think of is to increase it by a constant amount after each constant unit of time. The way David has things set up, it takes about two seconds for the bomb to drop. So (somewhat arbitrarily) David arranges his program so that the bomb's

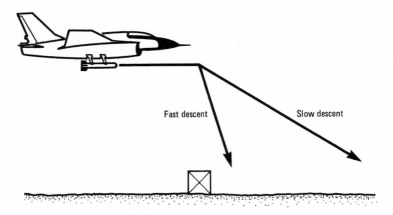

FIGURE 5.6

He improves it further.

downward speed increases by ten miles an hour after every half second. The bomb's path then looks as depicted in figure 5.7. Better, but still not perfect. Falling things change their direction of motion smoothly, not abruptly. So David tries increasing the speed every tenth of a second, and finally every sixtieth of a second, which is as fast as is permitted by the computer. At that point, the path looks like the one depicted in figure 5.8, which is at least in accord with David's vision of how it *ought* to look. A proud David has discovered in a day what it took Isaac Newton many years to figure out.

In the process of solving the bomb problem, David has reinvented Newton's first law of motion—that an object moving in a direction of motion will continue in that direction unless acted on by an outside force. Moreover, he has rediscovered the law that the force of gravity causes accelerated motion—that speed increases at a constant rate as a

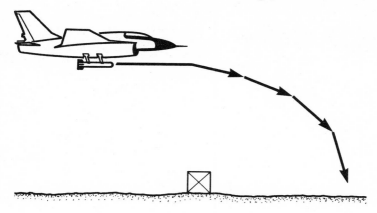

FIGURE 5.7

The naive physicist is rapidly losing his naiveté.

function of time. Perhaps David couldn't have stated these laws in this formal way—not yet, anyway. But, since he has, in a very real sense, invented them, he had a superb intuitive feeling for them. When David would eventually be introduced to the rules in a formal physics class, he would have very little difficulty understanding them because he had already internalized the concept.

In a famous Platonic dialogue, Socrates demonstrates that a naive learner actually has, inherent within him, the knowledge of the Pythagorian theorem. In a similar way, the preceding example indicates that David had the knowledge of physical law inherent within him—it only took a video game to extract it. By seeing the way things were hypothesized to happen, he was able to tell immediately whether the hypothesis was correct, and he was provided with clues about how to correct erroneous hypotheses.

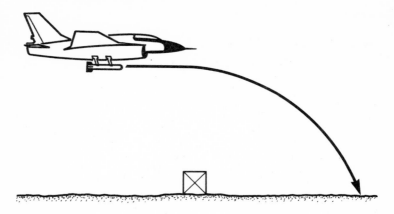

FIGURE 5.8

The proud physicist has discovered Newton's first law.

VIDEO REINFORCERS

No matter how sophisticated educational techniques become, it seems inevitable that there will remain *some* bodies of knowledge that will only be learnable through the kind of sheer, tedious repetition that will never be fun. There will always be orders of U.S. presidents to learn, irregular verbs to conjugate, and multiplication tables to memorize.

A possible use of video games for these wearisome chores is as a reinforcer. Remember from chapter 2 that reinforcers tend to increase the behavior that just preceded them. In many instances, learning and reinforcement can all be rolled into one neat and tidy educational package. Indeed, there now exist programs that will teach, say, spelling. After some number of correct responses, the spelling program suddenly vanishes and is replaced by a game of Asteroids. After the player has been defeated at Asteroids, back to spelling.

All the sophisticated and complex principles of reinforcement can be easily programmed into this kind of package. For instance, to get the student going on spelling (or verb conjugation, or proving geometry theorems) the program can provide continuous reinforcement—a video game following each correct answer. Gradually, then, the ratio of correct answers to video games can be increased until the student is on an efficient, partial reinforcement schedule. Later we'll discuss the possibilities for actually using this kind of technique in a video parlor to increase the amount of useful education that takes place there.

Direct Educational Benefits

Probably the question that we are most asked in connection with video games is: Do the kids learn anything useful by playing those crazy games in the arcades? As we've noted, the answer to this question is still open. There's one notable area in which research is being done and in which definite progress has been made. This is the area of video game therapy for various types of mental disorders suffered, for example, by people who have had strokes or automobile accidents.

Before getting into this area, however, we must inquire about educational benefits of video games for relatively untroubled people. Are there any? We asked a number of psychologists around the country what they thought—at least intuitively—about whether people learn from the games, and the answers ranged from "Maybe they're learning a tiny amount" to "Probably they're not really learning anything." The general consensus was that if a game was not really designed to teach

141

a specific skill, there was little likelihood that it would just happen to teach something useful.

What about motor coordination? If you skim through the video game magazines, you get the impression that we are, through the miracle of video games, becoming a nation of unsurpassed eye-hand experts—that our youth is acquiring priceless skills that, at a moment's notice, could be transferred to make them superb marksmen or air traffic controllers or athletes. But is this really true? Again, the answer is currently up for grabs, since the research has not been done. The psychologists we talked with were skeptical. "Practice in eye-hand coordination?" said one of our colleagues incredulously when we posed the question to him. "Every human being gets practice in eye-hand coordination every time he picks up a pencil or a pen! What additional benefit could playing video games have except maybe to make people better at playing other video games?"

Our own intuitions are a little more optimistic. Since the widespread introduction of television, we've been entering an age in which the way we do things—indeed the way we *think* —has shifted from a linear, logical mode to a more spatial, visual, global mode. (Marshall McLuhan, of course, pioneered this insight.) One very salient manifestation of this shift is the recent explosion in the use of computer graphics. Such graphics are becoming increasingly sophisticated and are finding their way into a wide variety of disciplines. An architect designing a new building, for example, can program a computer to display various versions of the building in different perspectives, thereby seeing in minutes a series of drawings that would have taken weeks in the precomputer days. Or an accountant, presenting a company's financial state, can do so by showing a series of computer-generated graphs and charts rather than reciting a long, dreary string of numbers.

The list of such examples is virtually endless. It is natural to ask, then, whether all the practice that today's video game players receive as they watch and manipulate shapes on screens is likely to help them in their later lives when they're using computer graphics daily. It's tempting to speculate that it might. On the other hand, any such help might better be classified as the indirect type that we considered earlier. Perhaps playing the video games will do no more than grease the path, so to speak, for learning the computer programming that will directly serve the future needs of today's young video game players.

It's noteworthy, in this respect, that the U.S. Army is currently considering video games as a means of training its recruits for the very similar task of learning to operate artillery. The army itself is remaining fairly quiet about this project, perhaps out of doubt that it will really work, or perhaps out of embarrassment over the image such a program might create in the minds of the public. But others aren't remaining quiet at all. Art Hoppe, a columnist for the San Francisco Chronicle, for example, has this to say:[10]

WORLD WAR VII

It was June 28, 1994. Aboard the U.S. Space Station Dreadnought, silently orbiting 248 miles over Washington, D.C., the grizzled colonel addressed the dozen young men who comprised the elite Special Zapping Force.

"Man your consoles, men," ordered the colonel grimly. "Intelligence says the Russians are launching World War VII."

It had all begun 12 years earlier with the fourth orbital flight of the Space Shuttle Columbia. For the first time, the shuttle's payload and purpose were more military than scientific.

"After all," said the general in charge of the Pentagon's space

[10]Arthur Hoppe, "World War VII," *San Francisco Chronicle*, 29 June 1982, p. 33. Copyright 1982 Chronicle Publishing Company. Reprinted by permission of the author.

program, "space is the modern equivalent of the 'high ground' that military leaders have for centuries sought out and exploited to their advantage."

So it was that the struggle commenced between American and Soviet forces to seize and hold the "high ground" of space.

Initially, the two sides were relatively equal and the battles nip and tuck. Each attempted to flood outer space with spy satellites, hunter-killer satellites which sought out and destroyed the spy satellites, and "shoot-back" satellites which could sense and explode approaching hunter-killer satellites.

World Wars III and IV ended in ties with space cluttered by lumps of metal and tangles of wire. But the military on both sides were happy planning and fighting their wars hundreds of miles above the surface of the planet. And the public was equally happy to keep them there.

Then, in 1989, the Dreadnought was launched and manned by the Special Zapper Force, each highly skilled young member equipped with a viewing console and laser beam. The Russians countered with a similarly armed Salyut 8 space station.

But World War V was strictly no contest. When it came to shooting down enemy satellites, the Russians were simply no match for the Americans, most of whom had devoted up to ten hours a day since the age of seven training for just such a battle.

Typical of their ranks was 21-year-old Sergeant Dick Deadeye, who had graduated from the prestigious Institute of Astrophysics and Video Arcade on a Pentagon scholarship of $100,000 or, more accurately, 400,000 quarters.

While young Americans had been preparing for war, Russian youth had been wasting their time on chess, calculus and pushups. After their disastrous defeat in World War V, the Kremlin launched a crash catch-up program in every Russian community featuring such devices as "Tractor Command" and "Won Ton Invaders."

But it was too late. In World War VI, they were beaten again with Sergeant Deadeye racking up a record 1376 enemy satellites in 27 minutes. Yet here they came again.

"Fire!" cried the colonel and the screens lit up with exploding satellites and missiles. Suddenly, they all went blank. Then on each appeared the same message:

"This is the Intergalactic Council. Your species has been found guilty of littering, loitering and disturbing the peace. We have dispatched our Political Action Committee Man to deal with you."

"It's a trick!" shouted the colonel.

"No, sir," said Deadeye. "Look out the port!"

Sure enough, from a corner of the universe emerged a gigantic, yellow, pie-shaped object with a single eye and a wedge-shaped mouth. Shifting jerkily this way and that, it one-by-one gobbled up all the satellites, Salyut 8 and approached the Dreadnought head on.

"Fire, Deadeye!" ordered the colonel. "Only you can save the human race from extinction."

"It's no good, sir," said Deadeye. He then uttered the tragic words that had already brought gloom to the hearts of all red-blooded Americans for a generation: "I'm out of quarters."

Something not so unlike Hoppe's comic fantasy may soon be a reality. The concept of war in space is becoming more real with every passing day. Even on the ground, artillery is now operated using laser aimers whose data are depicted on a computer screen. At the very least, it would be to the army's advantage to select as recruits young men and women who are proficient on the kinds of skills that are useful in such a high-tech environment. Indeed, actual video games are now being considered for just such a selection process. One example reports work done on behalf of the U.S. Navy Biodynamics Laboratory.[11] After extensive testing with the games of Air Combat Maneuvering, Breakout, Surround, Race Car, and Slalom, the researchers conclude that "In terms of availability, equipment, reliability, expense, and other practical considerations, the video games have many advantages . . . video games have considerable promise for performance testing and other applied contexts." In other words, those people who were good

[11]R. S. Kennedy, A. C. Bittner, Jr., M. Harbeson, and M. B. Jones, "Television Computer Games: A 'New Look' in Performance Testing," *Aviation, Space, and Environmental Medicine,* January 1982.

145

on these games would be considered suitable for various, quite similar, military activities.

So far, we have been rather tentative about the direct educational benefits of video games. One area in which their use for learning has been quite real, however, is as training aids for certain cognitive and perceptual-motor disorders.[12] These disorders can be found in patients who have been in accidents, have had strokes, or have simply been born that way. Such persons, it turns out, can often be trained so they can learn to lead more normal mental lives. Video games have recently been discovered to be superb tools for use in such training effort.

Let's first consider a simple example. Some people have disorders involving the muscles of their eyes. One of the authors (EL) was one such sufferer. The therapy required for this disorder was very simple: she had to work with a contraption that presented two dots to the eyes, and she was supposed to constantly stare at them. The dots could be moved farther and farther away to create the proper exercise for the eye muscles. At other times she had to simply look back and forth between two dots for hours on end. Although the therapy was effective in theory, it was so boring that she rarely could bring herself to actually do it. Many types of video games, however, require exactly the same kinds of eye movements but are orders of magnitude more interesting. Some modern sufferers are being treated in this far more interesting way; according to several, the process is far more enjoyable.

Video games are already in use for ailments that are substantially more serious than an inability to move the eyes together correctly. A good example is Jan, another of our composite

---

[12]W. J. Lynch, "TV Games as Therapeutic Interventions," Paper presented at the American Psychological Association, Los Angeles, 1981.

respondents. Jan is a typical teenager who couldn't wait to get her driver's license. On the morning of her sixteenth birthday she took her driver's test, passing it by a mere two points. On weekends her father let her drive his car. Then, one Saturday, less than two months after her birthday, she ran the car into a redwood tree. Although Jan survived the accident, she did suffer some brain damage. Her major problem seemed to be a rather unexpected inability to spell, a malady known to specialists as spelling dyspraxia. Jan, depressed after her accident, was unable to complete the spelling drills that had been ordered as treatment. Fortunately, her doctor had another idea. At a nearby hospital, Jan was put on a new kind of therapy—video game therapy. Twice a week she went to the clinic for this novel treatment, mostly playing "Hangman," a game that is particularly enjoyable in its video format. In "Hangman," one or two people guess letters in a word. If a correct letter appears, there is no penalty; if an incorrect letter appears, another portion of the "hangman" is added on. After only two months of playing Hangman regularly, Jan's problem was substantially relieved. By Christmas it was no longer noticeable. Again we can contrast the motivational aspects of video game therapy with the more traditional methods such as old-fashioned spelling drills.

Even relatively simple games such as Pong and Breakout demand careful visual searching and tracking. Games like Concentration are useful for memory problems in general. Concentration is a measure of visual memory in which one or two players attempt to match objects revealed by choosing pairs of squares. In the game the memory targets are not specific to English-speaking persons; thus it can be used with non-English-speaking populations. Games like Adventure, in which a player must find a "hidden" object while avoiding dangerous pitfalls like dragons and enemies, are useful for rehabilitating people who have problems with strategy and planning. And the sports games, like Basketball, Bowling, and Football, in which the premium is on quickness, accuracy, strategy, and alertness, are useful for people who have problems with eye-hand coordination, visual field, and tracking.

A number of therapists have opened centers throughout the U.S. that are dedicated to video game therapy. Therapists informally report that patients who are not motivated on many other types of retraining tasks are finding the games highly challenging and beneficial. However, there is not yet a great deal of published research in the area. One intriguing study involved twenty-five learning-disabled children between the ages of six and thirteen.[13] Subjects were tested both before and after heavy playing of a number of video games. The game sessions lasted approximately thirty minutes and were carried out at weekly intervals for twelve weeks. Dramatic improvements occurred. Specifically, children improved in their ability to perform a line-tracing task that tapped into motor ability and in a task of spatial visualization in which they had to match a missing block with a like-shaped contour. Further research is now underway to answer such questions as whether it is best for the children to engage in "structured" or in "free" video game training.

One interesting ongoing rehabilitation project is that of William Lynch, Director of the Brain Injury Rehabilitation Unit, at the Palo Alto Veterans Administration Center.[14] Lynch has begun collecting performance records on normal patients playing video games in order to develop standard score profiles, much like those used with personality or neuropsychological data. The performance records of brain-impaired patients can then be compared to these standards. With these

[13]Lynch, "TV Games."
[14]Lynch, "TV Games."

profiles, it becomes very easy for the therapist to provide the patient with ongoing feedback through therapy. In addition to the feedback, Lynch is finding an important benefit of these games: patients don't have to come to the clinic for therapy; rather, the therapist (that is, the game) goes to the patient's home. Lynch hopes to see not only new video game programs and more varieties of games, but especially more sophisticated home video game units, which will permit user modification or development of programs.

Lynch has found that many potentially useful games are too difficult to comprehend or physically difficult to manipulate for certain patients at the early stages of recovery. He sees a need for more choices in game difficulty or format to accommodate people with cognitive disabilities. The use of adaptive controllers, for example, could make video games available to quadriplegics or multiple amputees. The quality of future video displays will be considerably improved, and soon we will see training programs that can evaluate skills requiring three-dimensional perception in a more lifelike manner. With these advanced techniques, an entire simulated environment such as a room or a building can be brought into the clinic or the home. Lynch believes that efficient and economical treatment dictates a change in approach from the traditional one on one to a combination of individual, group, and automated techniques.

What Will the Future Bring?

There are two obvious future directions for video games as learning devices. The first is to endow games specifically designed for learning with the ultra-motivating character of the arcade games. As we have seen, this is already occurring to some degree, as research projects move briskly along on several fronts. On a theoretical front, work like that of Malone is aimed at identifying the characteristics of video games that make them motivating to begin with. And on an empirical front, work like that of Fredriksen is aimed at actually creating video game–like computer programs that will help promote specific cognitive skills.

The second direction is to somehow make arcade games more specifically educational. One step would be to have arcade games keep track of the performance of individual players and use this information to start players off at appropriate difficulty levels. From the players' point of view, this would save an expert the boredom of moving through the elementary levels before reaching the level that presents him or her with a reasonable degree of challenge. In addition, points could be presented both cumulatively and as an average number per game. From the manufacturer's point of view, games that don't present any challenge are bad because they eat up the game's playing time—it would be much more profitable to start a good player off at a more difficult level, thereby decreasing the total amount of time played for that quarter. And from the point of view of educators and parents, keeping an individual's history is a very helpful step in the process of making the games educational.

A potentially more difficult problem will be to persuade game makers to insert educationally beneficial elements into the popular arcade games. Perhaps the same civic groups that are trying to have video parlors outlawed could instead try to arrange community subsidies for arcade operators or game manufacturers, the amount being determined by the degree to which designated educational games are played. Or perhaps tax credits could be granted for companies developing demonstrably educational games. But what if educational games simply cannot be made as inherently compelling as the more traditional video games? In that case, good performance on an educational game could be rewarded by a free turn on any game in the arcade. Community funding of such a scheme would probably be minuscule compared to the education budget as a whole.

The Research Window

We have painted a rather rosy picture of computer games as potentially powerful educational devices. Not everyone is so optimistic. Mark Lepper, who seems to be generally in favor of the games, is nonetheless careful to enumerate some of the differing opinions about a variety of computer-related issues. He writes:

To proponents [of the games], the addition of motivational features [such as fantasy, plots, graphics, and sound effects] is expected to enhance attention and produce superior learning. To critics, the addition of these extraneous features seems more likely to prove distracting and impair initial learning. At the very least, from this second perspective, the use of such features should make learning significantly less efficient per unit of time invested.[15]

Lepper goes on to list similarly opposing opinions in other educational domains such as motivation and long-term retention.

Lepper raises other sobering issues as well about possible

[15]M. R. Lepper, "Microcomputers in Education: Motivational and Social Issues," Paper presented at the American Psychological Association, Washington, D.C., 23 August 1982.

social consequences of the games. We've noted that boys vastly outnumber girls in the video parlors and that computer games may well provide an easy lead-in to computer literacy. Like the Pittsburgh researchers cited in chapter 4, Lepper is concerned about the possibility of girls growing up to be second-class citizens where computer usage is concerned. And, he asks, what about class and socioeconomic differences? Will they be exacerbated due to the rich having greater access to computers than the poor? Or, conversely, will the video parlor prove to be a social equalizer in this domain?

These are serious questions, and, as Lepper points out, we don't have much time to answer them—we have a "research window" of perhaps ten years. To do the required research properly, it's important to be able to compare children who have had computer experience with other children who have not. But in the near future, it will be impossible to find research subjects who are computer-naive. That happened with TV. There was about a five-year period in the early 1950s when it would have been possible to match groups of TV-watching children and non–TV-watching children. Comparison of such groups would have allowed powerful conclusions about effects of TV on a variety of social and educational behaviors. But this opportunity slipped away. Before the social scientists realized what had happened, the vast majority of homes in the U.S. had a television set, and the opportunity to do the research properly had vanished forever. We hope, along with Lepper, that this missed opportunity will not repeat itself with computers because computers will probably have effects on our society more profound than those of television.

CHAPTER 6

THE COMPUTER CONNECTION

We hope that some of the readers of this book will follow the path from video games to computer technology, and it seems appropriate to end by sketching out for computer novices how computers operate, what the major trends are in the technology, and how computers broadly relate to the games.

The Computer as a System

To be a computer, a device must have two characteristics. First, it must be capable of solving problems by manipulating info-mation according to systematic rules. You mimic the principal operations of a computer when, for example, you multiply two three-digit numbers to find their product. The process is a sequence of logical, systematic steps such as elementary multiplication, carrying, and addition. Second, the device must be capable (at least in theory) of solving any problem that has a logical solution.

In chapter 3 we discussed a system as an integrated collection of components, all working in concert toward the accomplishment of some goal. Like a stereo system or a cognitive system, a modern computer is a system with at least three components: memory, a central processing unit (or CPU), and input/output (or I/O).

MEMORY

To store information, a computer has a memory made up of a long string of what are called words. Each word is actually a number. How many words are in a computer's memory depends on the computer, but memory typically comes in chunks of 1,024 words. When applied to memory size, this number—1,024—is, in computerese, called a thousand, or "one K." Thus a computer with 64K of memory would actually contain $64 \times 1,024$ or 65,536 words.

How does the computer keep track of what's where in its memory? Each location in memory has an address. The address of the first word is 0, and, in the case of a 64K computer, the address of the last word is 65,535 (that is, the 65,536 words are numbered 0 through 65,535.) The computer is able to access any of the words by its address. It can detect (or "read") the word at any given address and it can, in some cases, change (or "write") the word at a given address as well.

Computer memory is characterized as either "read-only memory" (ROM) or "random-access memory" (RAM). Read-only means just what it sounds like—the contents of memory are determined by the computer's makers when the computer is manufactured. The computer can read ROM—that is, it can determine what a word at some address in ROM is—but a ROM word cannot be changed.

Words that are in random-access memory, or RAM, can, in contrast, be both read and changed by the computer. Thus the essential difference between ROM and RAM is that the computer can change the contents of the latter but not of the former. Later we'll elaborate on the circumstances in which one type of memory versus the other tends to be used.

The numbers that constitute the words in a computer's memory can be used to represent information. This information can be of any sort, but two of the most common uses of words in memory are the representation of letters or other alphanumeric (keyboard) characters and the representation of video screen locations.

The numbers in memory represent letters when the computer is used as a "word processor" or computerized typewriter. For example, we are writing this book using a word processor. If one of us types the word "Information" on the computer's keyboard, each letter in the word is represented by a number, and as they are typed, these numbers are written into successive locations (addresses) in the computer's memory. Which numbers are used to represent which letters is arbitrary, but this correspondence was decided upon by an international committee some years ago, and it is called ASCII code. Table 6.1 shows the numbers that represent the letters in the word "Information." As one of us sits typing this manuscript, a long sequence of numbers goes into the computer's RAM, each number representing a letter (or some other keyboard character), and the sequence of numbers in the computer's memory thereby represents the manuscript we're writing. Eventually the numbers in all the memory locations that contain the manuscript will be sent, in sequence, to a printer. The printer is wired up so that when it is sent the number 73, it will print out "I," when it is sent the number 110, it will print out "n," and so on.

A second common type of information that the numbers in a computer's memory are used to represent are locations on a video screen. A video screen (of which a TV screen is a common example) is a tube, behind which (inside the TV) is a gun that shoots electrons. By aiming the gun at a particular place on the screen, that part of the screen can be displayed, or made to light up. In computer lingo, the location is "painted" on the screen. When used in conjunction with a computer, a typical video screen can be conceptualized as a grid, say 100 locations horizontal by 50 locations vertical. Each point in the grid (there are 100 × 50 or 5,000 of them in this example) is called a pixel, and the location of each pixel is specified by a horizontal and a vertical coordinate. For example (50,25) represents the pixel occupying the junction of the fiftieth column and the twenty-fifth row. (This would be the center of the screen, in our example.) An entire picture is painted on the screen by

TABLE 6.1
ASCII code

Letter	ASCII code representation
I	73
n	110
f	102
o	111
r	114
m	109
a	97
t	116
i	105
o	111
n	110

specifying a series of such coordinates and then aiming the electron gun so as to paint the corresponding pixels on the screen. Figure 6.1 shows how a flying saucer might be displayed. If you examined the figure carefully, you would find that 49 of the 5,000 pixels are painted—those at coordinates (51,24), (52,24), and so on.

The use of information in memory to represent locations on a video screen is, of course, critical in the construction of video games. It's the way Pac-Man, spaceships, and anything else appearing on the screen gets made. Soon we will expand this example to see in a little more detail how the computer might be programmed to display such a flying saucer and how the saucer might be programmed to do interesting things. Before we do this, however, a few words on computer programs in general.

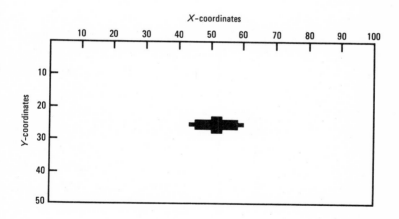

FIGURE 6.1

Close encounters of the computer kind: how a flying saucer might be displayed.

MIND AT PLAY

Earlier we pointed out that a necessary characteristic of a computer is flexibility—a computer must, at least in principle, be able to solve any solvable problem, and it must be able to manipulate information in any logically possible way. This flexibility is accomplished by a computer program, which is a list of instructions telling the computer what to do.

Computer programs reside in the computer's memory: just as the words in memory can be used to represent letters of the alphabet or locations on a screen, they can also be used to represent instructions in a computer program. For example, suppose you wanted to write some video game–related program. Starting simply, the first program you might want is one that would display the flying saucer depicted in figure 6.1. Figure 6.2, a schematic map of your computer's memory, gives the general idea of how the program works. The words at memory addresses 101 to 198 correspond to the coordinates of the pixels that are to be painted on the screen. The odd addresses (101, 103 . . . 197) contain the X (horizontal) coordinates, whereas the even addresses (102, 104 . . . 198) contain the corresponding Y (vertical) coordinates. Thus the words at a pair of addresses such as 101 and 102 contain the horizontal and vertical coordinates corresponding to one screen location that is to be displayed. For reasons that will become clear in a moment, location 199 in memory contains the number 255, which couldn't possibly represent an X or a Y coordinate (since X and Y coordinates have maxima of 100 and 50, respectively, in the hypothetical computer you are using).

Thus the information corresponding to the to-be-displayed screen locations are in addresses 101 to 198 of the computer's memory. How does the computer know what to do with them? Starting at address 1000 in memory, the words in memory

Address	Word	
0		
.		
.		
.		
101	51	
102	24	
103	52	
104	24	
.		
.		
.		Program
197	53	
198	28	1. Set V equal to 101.
199	255	2. Set X equal to word at address V.
.		3. Set Y equal to word at address V + 1.
.		4. Light up pixel at (X,Y).
.		5. Increment V by 2.
1000		6. Is the word at V equal to 255?
.		Yes: Go to Instruction 7.
.		No: Go to Instruction 2.
.		7. Stop.

FIGURE 6.2
The flying saucer program.

represent *instructions* that tell the computer what to do with the screen locations. Successive program instructions are put into successive memory locations. As it turns out, there is not one instruction per word—rather, each instruction uses more than one word. Exactly how words are assigned to instructions is beyond the scope of this book. All you need realize is that, starting at address 1000, the contents of memory represent instructions in a computer program.

This program has seven instructions. Instruction 1 says, "set some variable, V, equal to 101."[1] Instruction 2 says, "Set a

[1]More precisely, this means that the word at some as yet unused memory address (for example, address 5000) should be set to 101. Any subsequent reference to V is actually a reference to the word at address 5000.

second variable, X, equal to the word at address V." Instruction 3 says, "Set a third variable, Y, equal to the word at address $V + 1$." Instruction 4 says, "Display the screen location corresponding to X and Y." Instruction 5 says, "Increment V by 2." Instruction 6 says, "Is the value of the word at address V equal to 255? If so, go on to Instruction 7; if not, go back to Instruction 2." Finally, Instruction 7 says "Stop." You can now see the significance of the 255 at address 199. When the program finds this number, it will "know" that it has displayed everything to be displayed and that it is therefore finished.

This little program has demonstrated two major features of all computer programs. The first is a *loop*. The program loops between Instruction 6 and Instruction 2. Each time it goes through the loop, it reads another pair of X and Y screen coordinates from memory and paints the appropriate screen location. The second feature is *conditional branching*. This feature is embodied in Instruction 6, which says, "If one thing is true, then do something, whereas if another thing is true, do something else."

Once this program is written, and displaying the saucer, it would be relatively easy to extend the program so that the saucer appears to move. The extended program shown in figure 6.3, for example, would cause the saucer to appear to move to the right. Three instructions have been added in this program. Instructions 7 to 10 have the effect of incrementing all the X coordinates by 1. The program now loops from Instruction 10 back to Instruction 1. Every time it passes through the loop, all the X coordinates of the saucer are incremented by 1, so the saucer will be successively displayed one pixel to the right relative to where it had been displayed previously. The visual system will perceive a continuously moving saucer from these successive displays, just as it perceives continuous motion from the rapidly presented still pictures in a movie.

The program in figure 6.3 is still very primitive. Notice, for example, that the saucer will eventually disappear off the right-hand side of the screen. To see it again, you would have to restart the program. But most novice programmers would find it highly reinforcing to see even this much action occur as a result of a program they have written. If you understand the two simple programs we've provided so far, you can probably see ways to extend and improve them. For example, you might insert an instruction sequence that would detect whether the saucer was moving off the screen, and, if it were, to act accordingly—to move the saucer back to the left or, perhaps, as is so popular in video games, have it reappear somewhere else on the screen. By manipulating the vertical coordinates as well as the horizontal ones, you could have the saucer moving wherever you wanted on the screen. Extending the program still further, you might insert instructions to detect when something is

FIGURE 6.3

The flying saucer program extended.

1. Set V equal to 101.
2. Set X equal to word at address V.
3. Set Y equal to word at address V + 1.
4. Light up pixel at (X,Y).
5. Increment V by 2.
6. Is word at V equal to 255?
   Yes: Go to Instruction 7.
   No: Go to Instruction 2.
7. Set A equal to 101.
8. Increment word at address A by 1.
9. Increment A by 2.
10. Is word at A equal to 255?
    Yes: Go to Instruction 1.
    No: Go to Instruction 8.

typed in from the keyboard and have the saucer's behavior be contingent on what was typed in. Even with the simple sorts of instructions we've used, the possibilities are limitless.

In these examples, we've acted as if the program itself were humanlike in its ability to follow a set of instructions. The component of the computer that is actually responsible for carrying out the instructions is the central processing unit, or CPU. The CPU is the heart of the computer, and it has three major functions. The first is dealing with memory locations, which consists of both reading and writing (that is, changing the value of a word) at some memory address. The second function is communicating with the outside world. The third function is keeping track of the order in which program instructions should be executed. Generally, the CPU does this by assuming that it should execute instructions in the order that they appear in memory unless some instruction indicates otherwise. This kind of exception occurs, for example, in Instruction 6 in the program of figure 6.2. This instruction tells the CPU that, unless a particular thing is true (the value of V is 255), the next instruction to be executed is not Instruction 7 but, rather, Instruction 2.

INPUT/OUTPUT

So far we've focused on events that take place inside the computer. If a computer is to be useful, however, it must be able to communicate with the outside world. Such communication is called input/output, or I/O for short. Communication from the world to the computer is input; communication from the computer to the world is output. So, for example, displaying the Pac-Man board on a screen would be an output event —sending the locations stored somewhere in memory out to the screen. Detecting that the Pac-Man joystick has been moved would be an input event, in the sense that information from the outside world (the stick movement) would enter into the computer's CPU (which, in accordance with the Pac-Man program, would presumably then act in an appropriate way, that is, send output to the screen corresponding to the direction in which Pac-Man ought to move).

In the beginning days of computers—the late 1940s and early 50s—communication between the computer and the outside world was astonishingly primitive. Computers were used mainly as gigantic calculating machines, and computer programs were written primarily to solve tedious equations. At that time the only purpose of person-computer communication was to get programs into the computer and to read numbers that were the result of the computer's computations. These early computers had a row of lights on the console with a toggle switch under each light. Entering information into the computers was accomplished by setting the toggle switches in the appropriate configuration, and reading information from the computer was accomplished by reading the configuration of the lights.[2]

And so, by flipping toggle switches and reading lights, the computer pioneers would tediously enter data into the computer's memory, enter computer programs, and read the results of computations. It didn't take them long to tire of all this busy work, and soon the teletype, a remnant of the telegraph era, began to be used to enter data. The teletype looked like a typewriter with a long roll of paper feeding into it. The operator would type information into the teletype and, in addition to being printed out on the paper, this information would be

---

[2]The numbers within a computer's memory are actually represented in *binary*. In binary, each "digit" is either a one or a zero; thus a one was indicated by "switch up" or "light on" and a zero was indicated by "switch down" or "light off."

relayed electronically to the computer's CPU. Similarly, output from the computer would be transmitted from the CPU to the teletype, where it would be printed out.

The teletype was the major input/output device until about ten years ago. Even then it was clear that printing things out was the slow link in the system. Printing out took a long time, and it was unnervingly permanent. If you made an error, you couldn't erase it; you had to start again or somehow mark the error as such.

Today the almost universal form of basic human-computer communication is the video display/keyboard. The keyboard, like the teletype keyboard of yesteryear, is still used to enter information into the computer; however, the information is displayed not on a slow, permanent typewriter but on a speedy, easily erasable, and easily modifiable video screen. Whereas characters can be printed on a screen at the rate of hundreds, or even thousands, per second, even a very fast typist can type only about six or seven characters a second. Thus the slow link in the communications system has switched from output to input. The most likely new development in this area is that computers will soon be able to understand spoken speech, thereby improving things on the input side.

MASS STORAGE

We've noted that the primary virtue of a computer is its flexibility and that this flexibility is accomplished by the use of computer programs. More precisely, it is because any program can be run on any computer that this flexibility is available. In order to take advantage of the flexibility, we have to be able to run more than one program on any given computer. However, computer programs reside in computer memory, and computer memory, as we've seen, is limited. There's just so much information that can be stuffed into memory before you run out of room. This means that when we've finished with one computer program and want to use another, we'd like to have some place where we can easily store the program that we're done with. This is accomplished with mass-storage devices.

Mass storage was first done using IBM cards and paper tape. Most people are familiar with IBM cards. Essentially, they store information by having holes punched in certain places; the particular configuration of hole locations in the card represents the information. Paper tape worked similarly: holes were punched on a long strip of paper that looked like a roll 'of masking tape. When a person was finished using a computer program, the output from the program and, if necessary, the program itself were transferred via a computer-controlled punch onto tape or cards. When the information was to be fed back into the computer again, it was done via a card or tape reader.

These mass-storage techniques worked reasonably well, but they had two disadvantages. First, both punching the holes and reading the punched holes were slow processes. Second, piles of cards or long rolls of tape were inconvenient—they were big and bulky, and could easily get torn or, in the case of cards, dropped. This latter event was the nightmare of anyone who worked with computers, since it could take hours to reassemble a large deck of cards that had been accidentally dropped and scattered.

To rectify these problems, two other mass-storage devices were developed. The first is magnetic tape. Magnetic tape is simlar to video or audio recording tape, consisting of a long roll on which information can be stored in the form of magnetic impulses. Magnetic tape was convenient to use, but reading it and writing onto it was still a slow process. To get to wherever you want to be on the tape, you have to fast-forward or rewind it, which typically takes a long time.

The other device is the magnetic disk. A disk looks like a phonograph record, but its surface is covered with the same kind of magnetic material used on magnetic tape. Thus the physical storage of the information is the same on tape and on disk. The difference is that the disk is read or written on by the computer via a disk drive, which spins the disk very fast. The magnetic heads responsible for reading and writing can thus access any part of the disk—and any information on the disk —very quickly.

Computer Trends: Small and Fast

So much for an overview of what computers are designed to do and how they do it. We'd like now to take you on a more detailed tour of computer history. There are two major trends: computers are getting smaller, and they're doing things faster. These trends continue today; understanding them is very important if we are to be able to speculate about what the future has in store for video game technology.

CONCEPTUAL BIRTH

The idea of a computer came into being a surprisingly long time ago, courtesy of an eccentric but brilliant British mathematician named Charles Babbage. Babbage, who lived in the early 1800s, developed a fanatical dream to build a machine capable of solving polynomial equations. His principal motivation for this seemingly arcane cause was the same as every schoolboy's—he hated the tedium of performing this routine, boring task by hand.

Babbage managed to persuade Parliament to grant him £1,500—a princely sum—to develop what he termed a difference machine. And with this money, he actually succeeded in building a modest, but nonetheless working, version. In 1822 Babbage presented his invention to the British Royal Astronomical Society.

Impressive though it was, the difference machine was limited; all it could do was solve polynomial equations. Babbage wondered whether he could build a much more flexible machine that could be *programmed* to do a wide variety of tasks. Thus was hatched the idea of a machine able to do many tasks —indeed an infinity of tasks—depending on the sequence of instructions that it was issued. Babbage's remarkable intuition convinced him that such a machine was possible in principle,[3] and he got Parliament to advance him another £17,000 for this daring project. He proceeded to design the machine, which he named the Analytical Engine. The (very general) idea was that information would be represented by the relative positions of a series of gears—just as, for example, the number of miles an automobile has traveled is represented by a series of numbers on the odometer. The information would be manipulated— systematically changed—by changes in gears caused by changes in other gears. The machine itself looked like an enormous, Rube Goldberg-like hodge-podge of gears, cogs, cams, and other devices that had only just been invented.

Alas, Babbage's dream was never to become a reality. He worked endlessly on his analytical engine, but he could never get it to work right. The problem, although straightforward, was unsolvable: the technology of the time wasn't up to the task of building the components accurately enough. The finest machinists in England were incapable of grinding the levers and gears and cams to such a degree of accuracy that the whole, fantastically complex apparatus would lumber along smoothly.

[3]That it *is* indeed possible was later proved by another British mathematician, Alan Turing.

You can imagine Babbage's intense frustration. He felt, quite correctly, that if he could just get the machine to work, it would vastly diminish the burden of menial mental labor, just as the myriad inventions of the Industrial Revolution were vastly diminishing the burden of menial physical labor.

Babbage was a great visionary, and he must have died a disappointed man. But his ingenious design lay hidden like a land mine, waiting for the right combination of politics and technology to set it off a century later. It's a shame, really, that Babbage can't be brought back today to see the fruits of his ideas. Farsighted though he was, he would probably still be amazed to see his beloved machine shrunk to the size of a typewriter and responsible for everything from men landing on the moon to little, pielike humanoids zipping around mazes on mysterious screens in places where you drink your ale and buy your food.

THE ELECTRONICS EXPLOSION

Babbage's computer wouldn't work because it was fundamentally mechanical. Information was represented by moving gears, and the "CPU" was a similarly complex configuration of gears and cams. Whenever metal parts have to move in complicated patterns, extreme precision is needed. The whole thing was just too cumbersome.

By the middle of the twentieth century, more than a hundred years after Babbage's efforts, the electronic age was in full swing. Electricity provided the potential for incorporating Babbage's ideas into a workable device, since by using electrical components to represent information, the need for moving, mechanical parts could be vastly reduced. Additionally, manipulation of information could proceed very quickly when the manipulation consisted of on/off switching of electrical components rather than the movement of gears. In short, computers and electricity formed a potentially compatible partnership.

The arrival of World War II provided the final impetus for the creation of electronic computers. This war, like all others, spawned a variety of needs for sophisticated information-processing devices. One, for example, was the need to crack enemy communication codes. Additionally, new weapons were rapidly appearing on the scene, and complex computations were required to determine their performance characteristics. These needs led to a crash program in computer development, and in the 1940s, the first two computers—one, called the Mark I, built at Harvard, and the other, called ENIAC, built at the University of Pennsylvania—were turned on and actually worked.

These first working computers were huge, grotesque monsters, filling entire rooms. They were so big because primary informational components were vacuum tubes. Each tube is not that large—a few inches high and about an inch in diameter. But when you have thousands, each constituting only one tiny part of a computer's memory, the whole conglomeration takes up a lot of space.

These early, room-sized computers were useful for big, well-financed organizations such as the military, the census bureau, and a few large companies. But their use was limited—you could hardly put a bunch of them in a video parlor, for example. In the late 1950s, a major technological revolution occurred, one that rivaled in importance the invention of electricity itself. This was the invention of the transistor by a team of scientists at the Bell Telephone Laboratories. A transistor performs much the same duty as a vacuum tube, but it has three major advantages relative to a tube. First, it uses substantially less power. Second, it can be made arbitrarily small. And third, it operates a lot faster. The new generation of computers that used transistors in place of tubes arrived in the 1960s. They had

169

shrunk from the size of a room to the size of a piano, and they operated orders of magnitude faster.

A third revolution, which occurred in the 1970s, brings us up to the present. To get a flavor for this new development, it's important to realize that the first transistors, convenient though they were, still had to be manufactured individually and wired together in fantastically complex ways. One of us worked for a computer company in the mid-1960s and has vivid memories of platoons of middle-age women, sitting all day patiently threading wires together, looking as if they were all knitting a gigantic and incredibly intricate macrame plant holder.

This manufacturing bottleneck created problems as far as the finished product was concerned. First, another size limitation was soon reached, since the electrical wire that was used to string the transistors together couldn't get smaller than a certain minimum size, and, moreover, the individual components had to be large enough for the workers to manipulate by hand. Second, the workers themselves were expensive to employ, which meant that the resulting computers were similarly expensive. Third, since human workers—particularly those doing long, repetitious, boring jobs—make mistakes, the quality of the computers suffered.

All these problems ended with the development of the integrated circuit. An integrated circuit is a large number of transistors, miniaturized to a fantastic degree, all prewired and created in an instant on a single piece of silicon. The beauty of these integrated circuits, or "chips," is that once a master chip is designed and made to work, the creation of an indefinite number of copies is so cheap and easy as to be trivial—much as the making of an indefinite number of lithographs is trivial once the original plate has been made. Moreover, these chips can, in theory anyway, be made almost arbitrarily small. An entire computer CPU can now be placed on a silicon square the size of a fingernail, and they're getting smaller all the time. Indeed, if you've ever peeked inside a computer—or even a pocket calculator—you were probably startled to discover that it consisted mostly of air. That's because the actual electronic components are very small compared to the components such as keyboards, switches, and so on that are needed so that humans can operate the devices with their big, clumsy fingers.[4]

Special-purpose Computers

Thus far we have described the workings of what are referred to as general-purpose computers. The major characteristic of a general-purpose computer is flexibility, in the sense that any program can run on it. This means that all or most of the computer's memory is RAM, which, you'll recall, has the capability of being changed, or written into, as well as the capability of being read.

Increasingly, however, special-purpose computers are beginning to enter the world. As the name implies, a special-purpose computer is designed to do only one job. For example, you may have seen automobile advertisements featuring a "computerized fuel-injection system." Such a system involves a small computer that senses the state of a car's engine at each instant

---

[4]We are currently seeing a "multiple-use wristwatch" craze. Computer components are sufficiently small that tiny computers can be put into watches, which can then act as calculators, play popular tunes, and even display video games in addition to a myriad of timekeeping activities. But there is a serious limitation on these gadgets, which is the number of buttons, pressable by human fingers, that can be attached to them.

in time, computes the most efficient fuel/air ratio, given the temperature, air pressure, engine power, and so on at that instant, and then adjusts the fuel flow such that the appropriate ratio is obtained. As we shall see, arcade video games are special-purpose computers.

Since a special-purpose computer does only one job, only one program is required for it. This means that the program is written by the computer designers and put into read-only memory, or ROM, which, you'll recall, can't be modified. What's the advantage of this technique? The program can't be changed, either unintentionally or by mischievous hands. More important, it turns out that when a computer is turned off, the contents of any RAM disappears. Thus, with a general-purpose computer, some program has to be entered into the computer each time the computer is turned on, which requires a mass-storage device where the program can be stored when the computer is turned off. Such a requirement would be an unnecessary nuisance for a special-purpose computer, such as an arcade video game. This is why the program is stored in ROM, which is immune to the computer's being turned off. The program is part of the computer's basic electrical configuration, or hardware.

Does this mean that a special-purpose computer isn't really a computer, since we've defined flexibility—the ability to handle multiple programs—to be a necessary characteristic of a computer? The answer is yes and no. One can't *easily* change the program in a special-purpose computer. However, the ROM where the program resides is all placed on a single tiny chip that plugs into the computer proper. It's perfectly possible for the computer manufacturer (or anyone else) to write a new program, put it on a similar ROM chip, and replace the old chip. Thus even special-purpose computers are flexible enough to handle multiple programs.

Fundamentally, a video game consists of a computer program that somebody has written. Any *particular* video game can generally be run either on a special-purpose or a general-purpose computer. The video games that you see in video arcades or in other public places are almost invariably special-purpose computers. The most expensive and elaborate part of the arcade game is the video screen. The computer that runs the game is very small and relatively cheap.

Many video games also are made in versions that run on general-purpose computers, usually home computers. The video game programs for these general-purpose computers come on some mass-storage medium. For most inexpensive home computers, the mass-storage medium is a cassette of magnetic tape; thus the programs that you buy at your neighborhood department store are in the form of cassettes. More sophisticated (and expensive) home computers often have disk drives. Hence video games can also be stored on disks and sold as such. As with any general-purpose computer, the game program resides in RAM memory and must be read into the computer from the mass-storage medium whenever the game is to be played. The differences between special-purpose, arcade video games and those played on general-purpose home computers are interesting from a psychological point of view.

Home computers have a number of obvious advantages over arcade games. First, once you've purchased the computer (and the games themselves), the rest is free. But there's a more important advantage: if you're willing to learn how to program, you can create your own games or modify existing ones that you've bought. For many people, programming computers is an enjoyable, sometimes even addictive pursuit. However, learning to program is often a scary undertaking for the uninitiated, and strong motivation is necessary to get past the initial act of sitting down to write one's very first program. Programming a video game often provides this requisite motivation because the games are fun. In addition, it's fairly easy to write a very simple little program—often following some example given in a manual—and thereby to see instant results of your efforts and to have instant success.

However, if you play video games primarily because you like them, then, at least at present, arcade games are clearly superior to those designed for home computers. The designers of arcade games know that the games that are going to attract the greatest number of quarters are the games that are the most fun. So a lot of effort goes into making them fun. The designer of a general-purpose, home computer, in contrast, has different goals, and the games that are produced for these computers are incidental—they're just one of a number of products that are designed for the computers. The computer manufacturers have to spread their energies—they have to design their computers to be fast and general; the computers must be number manipulators, word processors, and a variety of other things. Since home computers are so much more varied, there's not quite the incentive to focus on making the game aspects of them as much fun as they possibly can be.

From a technical standpoint, there's a second advantage to arcade games, which is that each machine can be tailored to a specific game. Consider, for example, the differences between the home computer and arcade versions of Pac-Man. The arcade version is a wonder to behold. The gaudy design on its exterior is a delight (for video players, anyway). The joystick is the perfect device for controlling Pac-Man's motions. The screen is high quality and Pac-Man moves smoothly around on it. Most home versions are quite different. First, many home computers don't have joysticks associated with them, so Pac-

Man's motions have to be controlled with keys on the keyboard instead. This arrangement turns out to be considerably less satisfying. Second, the computer screen used by a home computer usually consists of the family TV set. While a TV may be adequate as a computer video screen, it is by no means ideal. You usually find that the image jiggles a bit, the focus isn't quite as sharp as you'd like it to be, and the color isn't quite right.

The Evolving Game

Computers are evolving astonishingly quickly. In *The Micro Millennium,* Christopher Evans provides the following analogy: if the automobile had made as much progress over the last thirty years as the computer industry, it would now be possible to buy a Rolls-Royce for roughly $2.75; it would get nearly 3 million miles to the gallon; and it would deliver enough power to tow an aircraft carrier.

Computer games, riding this wave of computer evolution, offer some tremendous advantages over their predecessors. By summarizing some of these advantages and by extrapolating the evolutionary process, we can speculate about where these games might be going.

ELECTRONICS

Computer games are devices that are almost completely electronic. There are few, if any, moving mechanical parts, which means that the games are easy to manufacture (and therefore relatively cheap). They are reliable; moving parts wear out, whereas electronic parts generally don't (or at least they wear out much more slowly). Therefore, it's much easier and cheaper for arcade operators to maintain them. Further, electronic parts operate extremely quickly, which means that games based on them can operate at very fast speeds.

PROGRAM FLEXIBILITY

But by far the greatest advantage of computer games is the flexibility inherent in the computer programs that go into them. To see the advantages of this flexibility, imagine that you wanted to make a realistic but noncomputerized space game. You would design what amounted to a small stage set, in which space-related objects such as asteroids, spaceships, and extragalactic creatures would appear from the wings, probably suspended by thin wires and propelled by some kind of motor-operated pulley system. Such an arrangement would be very difficult to manufacture properly and would also be extremely limited in terms of what it could do, how modifiable it was, and how realistic it would appear to be.

Such potential drawbacks, however, have apparently not deterred all game designers. On July 7, 1982, the Associated Press released an interesting news item that described a new type of game being unveiled at the Knoxville World's Fair. In this game, mechanical robots marched jerkily about in a boxing ring–like arena, shooting each other with "laser guns" and otherwise creating the same kind of havoc that ordinarily takes place on a video screen. The movements of the robots, along with the firing of their formidable weapons, are controlled by the game's players (who themselves remain safely on the side-lines, manipulating joysticks that "look just like a fighter pilot's"). According to its promoters, this game represents the next logical advancement over video games—a claim apparently based on the realistic, three-dimensional quality of the game. The promoters conceded that the game was expensive —around $200,000—but seemed undaunted.

Unfortunately for the promoters, their dreams are probably unrealistic, because this game represents a step backward from the computer technology that has made video games so successful. Instead of being electronic, the game is primarily mechanical, which means that there are the same slow, troublesome, error-prone moving parts that video games have managed to eliminate. The game's flexibility is woefully limited. To simply change the setting or the nature of the robots, for example, would be enormously costly and time-consuming. The three-dimensionality of the game is obviously an advantage, but it is really the only advantage.

With a computer/video system, in contrast, there is no foreseeable limit of how complex and how sophisticated such a game could be. Suppose, for example, that you wanted to simulate a player's disappearance into hyperspace, followed by the player's reappearance some time later in an entirely different region of space. Such a feat wouldn't have been possible with a mechanical game, but it isn't difficult to program on a computer. Such a program could be easily designed so that the player would appear to be in one region until he or she pressed the hyperspace button, at which time the screen would become filled with breathtaking special effects, corresponding to the programmer's vision of what being in hyperspace is like. Then a completely different region would be made to appear on the screen. In general, the rule is: Anything that can be imagined can be programmed. And, surely, to be limited only by imagination is the ultimate in game design flexibility.

The greatest benefit of this flexibility is clearly the enjoyment the player can potentially get out of playing the game. But there are other, less obvious benefits that accrue to the arcade operator who is primarily interested in making money. It turns out that, with many arcade games, the program that runs the game is also designed to do convenient things for the operator. For instance, have you ever noticed what a game does when no one is playing it? Sometimes it just sits there doing nothing, whereas other times it mimics what happens when the game is actually being played. An idle Pac-Man machine, for example, sometimes has just the Pac-Man logo on it; other times Pac-Man is moving aimlessly back and forth; and still other times, what appears to be an actual game is going on. What determines when a machine does what? The game is programmed to do any one of a wide variety of things when it's not being played. Which thing it *actually* does is under the control of the operator. By changing the position of a switch inside the machine (accessible only to the operator), the program will be changed so as to do one thing or another. Thus the operator can perform little experiments to find out which of these "idle-time" activities will provide the most effective come-on for clientele. And this idle-time option isn't the only thing that the operator has under his or her control. Most people realize that the games (actually the programs) keep track of what the high scores are for that game and display the high scorers' initials. What's not so well known is that a game can keep track of many other things as well: how many quarters have been inserted into it, the average length of playing time per quarter, the number of times the various levels of difficulty have been achieved, and anything else the operator might want to know about. All this information is available to the operator and can be displayed on the screen whenever he or she wants to see it.

Moreover, many games have variable difficulty. By changing the position of another switch, a game can be made more easy or more difficult. This provides the operator with a defense if the arcade starts to become frequented by especially expert players.

Let's see how difficulty might be manipulated with Space

Invaders. In this game, aliens drift across the upper part of the screen, and during each successive short period of time (say every second) an alien will drop a bomb with some probability. Suppose, for example, that the per-second probability of dropping a bomb is to be one in five. This means that every second, there's a one-fifth probability that a bomb will be dropped or, on the average, a bomb will be dropped once every five seconds.

How does the program accomplish this, that is, what determines the bomb-dropping probability? Part of the computer program that constitutes the game of Space Invaders is what's called a random-number generator, which, as the term implies, generates a random number each time one is requested by the program. Suppose the random numbers generated by the generator range from one to ten. This means that if you choose a random number, the probability is one-fifth that the number selected will be two or less (that is, that it will be a one or a two). Somewhere in the program will be a sequence of instructions that goes:

1. Set some variable, X, to 2.
2. Choose a random number (between one and ten).
3. If the number is X or less, drop a bomb. Otherwise don't drop a bomb.

This little sequence of instructions (which is called a subroutine) will be executed every second.

Suppose you want to make the game more difficult. One way would be to boost the per-second probability of dropping a bomb from one-fifth to one-half (which would mean that, on the average, a bomb would be dropped every two seconds instead of every five). To make this change in the program, all you have to do is change the "2" in Instruction 1 to "5." The same general principle holds for other changes in video game difficulty. It is in the nature of computer programs that making a tiny change in the program can have a profound effect on what the program does.

THE TECHNOLOGICAL FREE RIDE

The third major advantage enjoyed by computer games is that they are yoked to computer technology: many of the new developments stemming from computers have direct spinoffs in video game technology. As computers become faster, cheaper, smaller, and more convenient, so will the associated games. As video screen technology becomes more advanced (incorporating, for example, holographic or highly realistic 3D effects), these features can be immediately incorporated into video games.

To provide just one concrete example, consider the fabulous special effects that are now being used in filmmaking (for example, in the *Star Wars* series). These effects are now almost exclusively generated by computers, and an awful lot of money has been spent to develop them. A game manufacturer may not have the resources to develop these effects, but since they've already been developed by moviemakers, it's not difficult for the game designers to use the technology and transfer it over to games.

Video games are evolving very fast. The primary reason for this is that the computer technology that underlies them can be easily modified. In the old days, if a game didn't seem to be quite right, that was too bad; the cost of changing it was too great to be worthwhile. To change a computer-based game, in contrast, all one has to do is to modify the program.

A second reason for the rapid evolution of the games is that technological innovations are happening very quickly. Graphic quality, for instance, is of primary importance to video game addicts. Zaxxon is not considered to be particularly good as a game per se, but it's nonetheless popular because of its superb graphics. Computer technology is rapidly advancing in graphic resolution and graphic realism. Resolution refers to the inherent quality of the image. Contrast, for example, a photograph in a magazine like *National Geographic* with a photograph that appears in a newspaper. Most images—both those that are printed and those that are displayed on video screens—are made up of a large number of small dots (which, you'll recall, are called pixels when they are locations on a video screen). The smaller and more densely packed the dots, the better looking is the image. In a newspaper photograph, the dots are large enough to be seen with the naked eye, whereas in *National Geographic*, the dots are microscopic.

High resolution is desirable in video games. First, a higher-resolution image fundamentally looks better. Second, the higher the resolution, the more lifelike the characters can be; with low resolution, the best you can do is to make stick-figure-like characters. And, finally, with high resolution, the appearance of motion is better. With low resolution, motion looks jerky and unrealistic; with high resolution, it looks smoother and more realistic.

Currently, most video screens (particularly home video screens) are more akin to newspapers than high-quality magazines. As you look at the screen, you can actually see the dots that comprise the image. But this is changing. Very high resolution graphics already exist, and as their price comes down, we will see them used more and more in video games. We won't take the time here to go into a detailed description of the technology behind high resolution. Suffice it to say that it is highly dependent on computer speed; in general, the faster a computer can operate, the more points it can paint on a screen within a given period of time and the higher the resolution can be.

Graphic realism refers to the degree to which the image looks realistic. In large part realism is determined by the degree to which the image is made to look three-dimensional rather than two-dimensional. Pac-Man, for example, is a two-dimensional game; it has a "flat" board with "flat" Pac-Men. In Zaxxon, on the other hand, objects are depicted in three dimensions—a three-dimensional aircraft swiftly weaves its way through a gauntlet of three-dimensional obstacles—and it is this graphics feature that has been lauded by the video players.

If three-dimensional graphics are so much better than two-dimensional ones, why aren't all games three-dimensional? The reason is simple: it's much harder to write computer programs that depict things in three dimensions. Two-dimensional graphics, in contrast, are (quite literally) child's play. However, this situation is rapidly changing as well. Computer programming ("software development") is a subject of intense research these days, and one of the fruits of this research is better knowledge of how to write three-dimensional graphics. Like high-resolution hardware, three-dimensional software is beginning to trickle down to the domain of video games.

A Final Note

On November 9, 1982, the U.S. Surgeon General, Dr. C. Everett Koop, delivered a speech in Pittsburgh during which he declared that video games were evil entities that produced "aberrations in childhood behavior." Koop went on to urge that video games not be played.

Not since King Canute ordered the tides to recede has an edict been issued that is destined to have less effect on its audience. Because of psychological principles that are well understood, video games are likely to last. Further, as we've seen, the games can rapidly adapt to popular moods and fads and interests. They aren't going to disappear just because the surgeon general or anyone else has commanded them to.

Moreover, video games are actually in a position to provide society with very substantial benefits. As we noted in chapter 5, video games could be implemented for educational purposes in at least three different ways: specially designed games could be run on the computers that already exist in many schools, educational games could be marketed for home computer, and video game systems and games in arcades could be modified to include educational features.

Surgeon General Koop is not alone in his antipathy toward video games. We've seen parents and other authorities exhibit enormous fear and loathing toward video games and especially video game arcades. This antipathy has resulted in individual attempts to ban offspring from playing games and in collective attempts to ban video games from communities. And yet, as we've seen, the games have enormous potential as teaching devices. We've touched on only a few of the possibilities in this book; we've only scratched the surface. At a recent (May 1983) Harvard conference, "Video Games and Human Development," for example, researchers presented positive findings about effects of video games on everything from medical rehabilitation to cognitive and problem-solving skills to social behavior. One participant reported that video game players, contrary to popular views, are relatively high academic achievers. It should be noted that there were no critics of the games at this conference, and, of course, in any very new area of study, results should be interpreted cautiously. Nevertheless, rather than expending vast amounts of energy on prohibitive measures that seem doomed from the start—kids are going to play video games one way or another just as they will read comic books or furtively flip through *Playboy*—it seems much more sensible to expend the energy in harnessing the educational potential. That's really our only strong editorial stance about video games.

INDEX

Index

Binary numbers, 163n
Bolt, Beranek and Newman, 126
Bomber Pilot, 6
Brain-impaired, video game therapy for, 148–49
Brain Injury Rehabilitation Unit, at Palo Alto Veterans Administration Center, 148
Breakout, 34, 35, 70, 145; object of, 34–37; as video game therapy, 147; visual destruction as reward, 37
British Royal Astronomical Society, 167

Carlsmith, J. M., 27
Central processing unit (CPU), 154, 168; and computer programs, 158–62; three major functions, 162
Challenge, 41–42, 126, 127; computer interaction, 118; variable difficulty level, 42
Chunk(s), 79
"Cocktail party phenomenon," 46
Cognitive dissonance, 26–29; enjoyment and cost, 29; extrinsic v. intrinsic reinforcement, 28
Cognitive system, 43, 44; components, 45–63; environmental stimuli, 48; reaction time, 55
Cohen, Harold, 111
Collective behavior, 92–97; analyses of, 93; spread of, 95
Community funding, 151
Competition, video game, 5
Computer(s): conception, 166–68; electronics explosion, 168–71; first, 169; general-purpose, 171; graphics, 119, 142; as interactive devices, 116–21; introduction to, 122–25; programming, 120, 123–25, 173; special-purpose, 171–75; use of, in education, 116–21
Computer as a system: input/output, 162–64; mass storage, 164–66; memory, 154–57

Computer-assisted instruction (CAI), 116; advantages of, 118; availability of, 119; benefits of, 117; effectiveness of, 121; lack of usefulness, 118–19; problems, 118–19; and regular instruction, comparison of, 118; resource problems, 119
Computer control, in video games, 7
Computer evolution, 175–82; electronics, 175–76; program flexibility, 176–80; technology, 180–82
Computer programming, 120, 123–25, 173; advantages of learning, 120; learning, 120; physics, 134, 135–39
Computer revolution, 106–7
Computer technology, 96
Computerese, 154
Concentration, 147
Conditional branching, 160
Conditioning, see Reinforcement
Continuous reinforcement, 16, 20
Craze, 94
Crimes, video game-related, 109–10
Curiosity, 42

Danger, and excitement, 32
Darts, 34, 37, 40, 129; object of, 37–39
Death and destruction, in video games, 5–7
Death Race, 102
DeCordova Museum, 110–11
Defender, 51, 54, 80, 101; eye-hand coordination, 121
Den of male culture, 105; consequences of, 106
Designing new games, 80–82; "Ground-level Pac-Man," 81–82
Difficulty, in video games, 20–22; challenge and, 42; levels of, 127
Digital computer, 5
Donkey Kong, 45, 46, 54, 100, 101
Drill-and practice program, 117, 118
Dungeons and Dragons, 32

Index

Index